THE GREAT
GENESEE ROAD

Of the Genesee Road's many bridges across rivers and creeks in its three hundred plus miles, the grandest was surely the 1806–1808 span over the Mohawk at Schenectady designed by Theodore Burr, a cousin of Vice President Aaron Burr. Three massive stone piers carried the road on a series of arches for 997 feet. Although they were enclosed, over time the spans began to deteriorate and sag. More piers were added, eventually resulting in an undulating ride. Fifty cows fell through a rotted section of deck in 1857. A 1902 history of Schenectady recalled "in its old days a ghostly, ghastly tunnel over the river—it could only be described as spooky. Managerie elephants sometimes would not cross. . . . The cavernous old structure, as might well be imagined, was invested and infested at night by all the dissolute and disreputable vagabonds of both sexes in the city." The bridge was torn down in 1871. *New York Public Library.*

THE GREAT GENESEE ROAD

Traveling through Time on New York State's Historic Route 5

RICHARD FIGIEL

BOOKS

NORTH COUNTRY BOOKS

North Country Books
An imprint of The Globe Pequot Publishing Group, Inc.
64 South Main Street
Essex, CT 06426
www.globepequot.com

Distributed by NATIONAL BOOK NETWORK

British Library Cataloguing in Publication Information Available

Library of Congress Cataloging-in-Publication Data

Names: Figiel, Richard, author.
Title: The Great Genesee Road : traveling through time on New York State's historic Route 5 / Richard Figiel.
Other titles: Traveling through time on New York State's historic Route 5
Description: Lanham, MD : North Country Books, [2024] | Includes bibliographical references and index. | Summary: "Featuring rich storytelling, generous illustrations, historical and contemporary photographs, and detailed maps old and new, The Great Genesee Road is a fascinating trip through the making of New York State, the expansion of a young country, and a piece of history that readers can still explore today"—Provided by publisher.
Identifiers: LCCN 2024010625 (print) | LCCN 2024010626 (ebook) | ISBN 9781493075577 (paperback) | ISBN 9781493075584 (epub)
Subjects: LCSH: New York State Route 5 (N.Y.) | Genesee Road (N.Y.) | New York (State)—Description and travel. | New York (State)—History.
Classification: LCC F127.M55 F54 2024 (print) | LCC F127.M55 (ebook) | DDC 974.7—dc23/eng/20240517
LC record available at https://lccn.loc.gov/2024010625
LC ebook record available at https://lccn.loc.gov/2024010626

Contents

Timeline of White Settlement in Central/Western New York

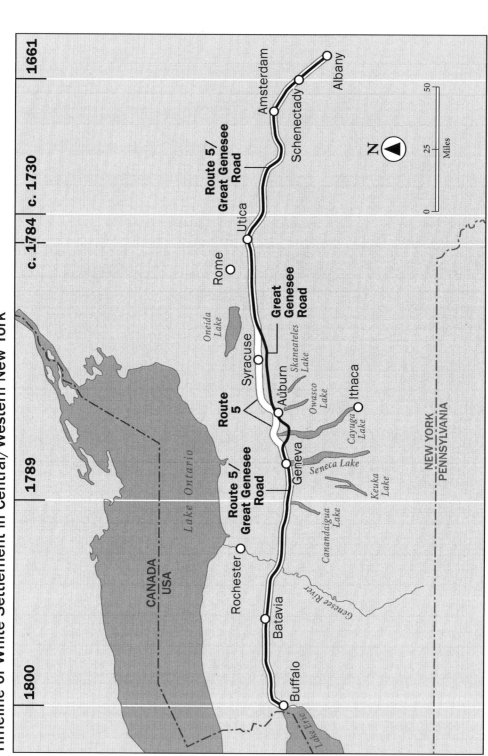

Prologue

A Captive Princess

In 1784, a year after the end of the War of Independence, a magistrate named Hugh White left Middletown, Connecticut, with his large family and all their belongings, headed for lands opening to settlement in New York State. The lure of "new land" was in full play throughout lower New England. The Whites made their way to Albany, then followed a cart track up the Mohawk River past a string of fortified houses and frontier settlements ravaged in decades of raids by French, Native Americans, British, and Tories.

Judge White brought his family into the Mohawk Valley as hundreds had before him and thousands would soon after, but he pushed on further than the rest, choosing a site beyond the ford across the Mohawk, near the mouth of Sauquoit Creek. It would later become the village of Whitestown, now a suburb of Utica. The family cleared a few acres, stacking felled trees into a log house and barn and attempting to befriend their neighbors, Oneida people living in the surrounding woods.

Family lore tells us that one morning while the judge was away, a party of Oneidas appeared on the Iroquois Trail from the west. Mrs. White offered them food. After awhile one of them, with the bearing of a chief, gestured for permission to take her youngest daughter on a visit to his home. The poor woman was speechless, as afraid to refuse as she was to assent. As the Oneidas stood waiting in their patient way, Hugh White returned home. When he heard the chief's request he immediately agreed, and off the girl went into the forest, dragging her mother's heart behind.

The hours must have passed slowly. Just as darkness set in, the Oneida party returned with the girl skipping beside them, decked out in deerskin and feathers. Taken off possibly as a captive, she returned an Indian princess.

The story may be apocryphal; admittedly it sounds a bit "Disney." But still, it seems a useful parable for the collision of cultures—the uncertainties, trusts, and mistrusts—that played out as white settlement creeped west along the Iroquois Trail, soon to become "The Great Genesee Road." Missing from the story was the theft of land, and all that entailed.

1

"A Fine Sandy Cart Road through Evergreens"

Not much more than a foot wide but worn smooth and deep—sometimes more than a foot deep from the tread of centuries—the Iroquois Trail was "main street" for the most powerful, organized Native American society in eastern North America. At its apogee in the seventeenth century, the sphere of influence of the Iroquois Confederacy—the Haudenosaunee Longhouse—extended from the mid-Atlantic region to Hudson's Bay and from the Hudson River through the Ohio Valley.

A central path through the Haudenosaunee homeland ran from present-day Albany to Schenectady, then along the north bank of the Mohawk River to cross at a shallow ford (Utica), continuing overland past ancient salt springs (Syracuse), skirting northern tips of Finger Lakes to the Genesee River (at Avon) and on to Lake Erie at Buffalo Creek. The trail bound together territories of the confederacy's five nations—from east to west, the Mohawk, Oneida, Onondaga, Cayuga, and Seneca. The Tuscarora joined as a sixth member nation when they fled north from Carolina territory. Representatives from each nation traveled this path regularly to the Great Council Fire kept by the Onondaga.

At its eastern end on the Hudson, the Iroquois Trail left the river at what is now downtown Albany and traveled northwest to the Mohawk River. The Iroquois called this *skahnehtati*, "beyond the pines," where they portaged canoes through the area's pine barrens, bypassing rapids and falls on the Mohawk. This portage surely dated back well before the time of the Iroquois when Algonquin people ruled the region.

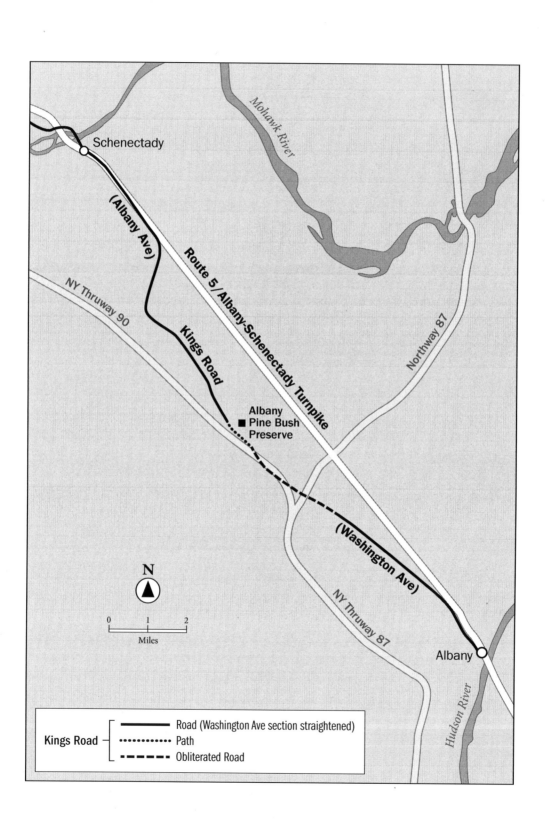

Schenectady

Mohawk River

(Albany Ave)

Route 5/Albany-Schenectady Turnpike

NY Thruway 90

Kings Road

Northway 87

Albany
Pine Bush
Preserve

(Washington Ave)

NY Thruway 87

N

0   1   2
Miles

Albany

Hudson River

Kings Road ⎯ ⎯⎯⎯ Road (Washington Ave section straightened)
.... Path
⎯ ⎯ ⎯ Obliterated Road

The historical record generally starts in 1609 with first contact between Native American residents and the river exploration of Henry Hudson. "The people of the Countrie came flocking aboard" Hudson's Dutch-sponsored ship *Halve Maen*, described in first-mate Robert Juet's journal, "and many brought us Bevers skinnes, and Otters skinnes, which wee bought for Beades, Knives and Hatchets." The Hudson River fur trade had begun. The next year, another Dutch ship arrived loaded with trading goods. The Dutch West India Company then established a trading post at the portage-head of the Iroquois Trail, the genesis of the colony of New Netherland.

Europeans arrived at a time when the Haudenosaunee were still expanding their territory, forcing Algonquin-speaking Mahican people from land west of the Hudson River. The people boarding the *Halve Maen* were Mahicans, and the Dutch began dealing with both Mahicans and Mohawks, but the principal fur trade soon followed the trail west into Mohawk and Iroquois country.

In 1970, excavation for Albany's Expressway 787 began turning up a trove of artifacts at an intersection with Routes 5 and 20: lead shot, glass beads, bricks, tiles, cannonballs, tobacco pipes, wampum. Archeologists confirmed this as the site of the Dutch Fort Orange trading post, uncovering remains of walls, a moat, houses, and a tavern. What could be salvaged was taken to the Crailo Museum across the river in Rensselaer. The rest was reburied seventeen feet under the expressway, at the epicenter of downtown Albany's garble of highway ramps. Here the Iroquois once brought bundles of beaver pelts, giving the name Beverwyck to a village of tradesmen attaching to the fort along the path rising from the riverbank, now State Street—the beginning of NY Route 5.

The only hint today of Hollanders who once called this *Joncker Straet* is a striking, faux-Dutch, stucco building used in recent years as a restaurant. It was designed in 1907, with a nod to the city's past, for the ticket office of the Hudson River Steamship Lines. Their boats docked at the end of the street where bark canoes once beached.

This part of downtown Albany is sprinkled with historical signs and plaques noting early Dutch and English building sites. One of them marks the location of *Beverwyck*'s municipal hall, the **Stadt** House, where early trade negotiations took place with the Iroquois. It was rebuilt by the British in 1740 for Albany's first city hall, but it was still called the Stadt House, as the language spoken in Albany remained principally Dutch throughout most of the eighteenth century.

In the summer of 1754, a congress of delegates from seven American colonies met at the Stadt House to try sorting out troubled relations with Native Americans, particularly the Iroquois, and to address related threats posed by French Canada.

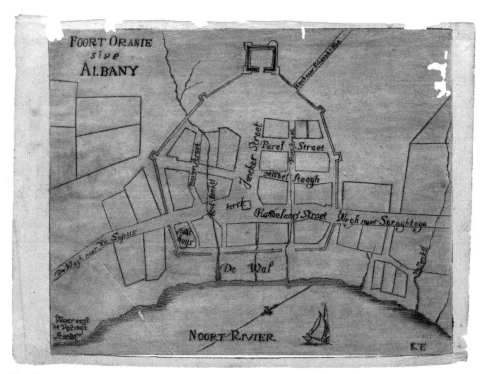

The Ten Eyck map of Albany, drawn around the turn of the eighteenth century, shows the road to Schenectady leaving a stockade gate near the fort still bearing the Dutch name *Foort Oranie* (Orange). At this time the little town had been part of the English province of New York for decades, but the language of Albany remained Dutch well into the 1700s. *Map courtesy of the Albany Institute of History & Art.*

Benjamin Franklin was one of the delegates from Pennsylvania. He was the key author and proponent of what became known as the Albany Plan, "a Proposed Union of the Colonies." It called for "one General Government in America" with power shared between a grand council legislative body, elected by the various colonial assemblies, and a president-general appointed by the crown. It was a first, tentative step toward autonomy for the North American colonies.

Franklin was familiar with the structure of the Iroquois Confederacy, and the proposed grand council was not unlike the councils of the Haudenosaunee Six Nations. "It would be a strange thing," declared Franklin, "if Six Nations of ignorant savages should be capable of forming a scheme for such an union, and be able to execute it in such a manner as that it has subsisted ages and appears indissoluble; and yet that a like union should be impracticable for ten or a dozen English colonies."

At the time of the Albany Congress, Benjamin Franklin published this woodcut political cartoon in his newspaper the *Pennsylvania Gazette*, hoping to stir public sentiment behind his proposal for colonial unity. The snake has only eight segments: the New England head represented that region's four colonies, Delaware is missing because it was still part of Pennsylvania, and Georgia was omitted presumably because it was so far from immediate concerns about the Iroquois Confederacy and French Canada. *Library of Congress.*

"A strange thing," but true. While the delegates at the congress unanimously approved the Albany Plan, their colonial legislatures either ignored or rejected it—a potential threat to their power, and a first test of American federalism. The king also said no.

At the site of the Stadt House, State Street passes through the phantom main gate that led into the stockaded English village of Albany. Years of devastating spring floods had nudged settlement from the proximity of the Dutch riverbank-fort onto higher ground. About where Broadway splits from State Street, two great Native American paths diverged, one running north along the Hudson, the other west to the Mohawk River Valley. Both were conduits for the torrent of beaver, otter, and other pelts coming out of the wilderness. The fur trade peaked in 1656, when more than forty thousand pelts left Hudson River docks, but shipments continued for more than a hundred years as animal populations were depleted deeper into the interior woods. At first the Iroquois brought their pelts to Beverwyck in pack-baskets or on sleds made from saplings lashed together, typically dragged along the trail by women, slowly smoothing and widening the footpath into what became a Dutch cart road. When the English took over, that roadbed was upgraded again to what was then declared the King's Highway.

As it climbs toward New York's Capitol building, State Street passes St. Peter's Episcopal Church at the corner of Lodge Street. This was the site of a new fort built by the English in 1676 to replace abandoned, crumbling, flood-ravaged Fort Orange. The route of the trading path continued through the hilltop fort to a back gate located

In downtown Albany, this sign roughly marks the place where the road to Schenectady—called "Kings Road" by the English—left Albany's palisade wall through a northwest gate. The sign is located at the corner of Eagle Street and Corning Place across from Capitol Park, with one tower of the Capitol building visible in the distance. *Photo by the author.*

at the edge of today's East Capitol Park. There is little doubt that New York State's Capitol building sits atop the Iroquois Trail.

Designed in large part by H. H. Richardson, the monumental Capitol took thirty-two years to build, beginning in 1867. Limestone came from the same Champlain Valley quarry supplying stone for the Brooklyn Bridge, under construction at the same time (but completed in less than half the time). Roads were diverted around the Capitol. Washington Avenue now takes over from State Street to approximate the route of the old trail through and out of the city.

Arrow-straight Washington Avenue leaves to the imagination any sense of a winding path. History addicts have used very early maps to plot old meanderings against today's road grid, but all efforts vanish when the avenue encounters the octopus of a Thruway/Northway/Route 90 interchange.

This is the edge of the Albany Pine Barrens Preserve, an extraordinary, 3,350-acre patchwork of lightly forested sand dunes between Albany and Schenectady. It is said to be one of the largest of only twenty inland pine barrens in the world; areas of infertile, sandy soil with open stands of pine and scrub oak scoured by periodic fires. When the trail and the Dutch and English road passed through here, the barrens were eight times the size of the preserve, continuous from the outskirts of one colonial village to the next.

A rare chance to experience the old road comes near the preserve's visitor center on New Karner Road. Many trails start from the center. One of them takes an unlikely direction toward the roaring NY Thruway, dips under the New Karner Road bridge over the Thruway, and heads northwest toward Schenectady. Coming out from under the bridge, the preserve's trail noticeably widens, looking more like a cart path or primitive road headed into the woods. This is indeed a surviving piece of the King's Highway, likely following the ancient Native American portage trail. For about a mile it is still the same "fine sandy cart road" described by Dutch travelers Jasper Dankaerts and Peter Sluyter in 1680, "through a woods of nothing but beautiful evergreen or fir trees"—never paved or traveled by an automobile. Following the American Revolution it became the Great Genesee Road.

The dirt road becomes paved as it resumes the original way to Schenectady with a historical sign noting "Kings Road." It continues past pine woods and a mostly rural landscape. By the mid-1700s this remote road became notorious for highway robberies, fur-smuggling, and darker deeds. The sandy land was unfit for farming, remained uncleared and uninhabited except for a few taverns. One of these, located about halfway between Albany and Schenectady, was run by Isaac Jacob Truax, vari-

The uncommonly sandy soil of pine barrens between Albany and Schenectady discouraged farming and settlement throughout the seventeenth and eighteenth centuries. The area's reputation as a haven for bandits and murderers didn't help. When turnpike alternatives came along in the early nineteenth century, the Kings Road was all but abandoned. In the early 1900s, a growing appreciation of the pine barrens' unique ecology inspired a movement to create a preserve. The Albany Pine Bush Preserve now protects more than 3,300 acres with 20 miles of trails. Among them is a mile-long piece of the Kings Road much as it looked when Dutch carts began using the Native American portage. *Photo by the author.*

ously described in local lore as "jolly good . . . very eccentric" and given to "fastidious and gaudy dress." During the Revolution the road between villages was a hotbed of Tory sentiment. Isaac Truax's Tavern became a meeting place for Loyalists, where occasional travelers were rumored to disappear. An excavation of the tavern site in the 1970s found human skeletons in the cellar, but the family itself rests in a little cemetery nearby in the woods. Roadside historical signs mark the locations. More than twenty signs were put up along Kings Road by Albany's city archaeologist in 1975.

After the Revolution, a migration of settlers (including Connecticut judge Hugh White) began to stream through Albany headed west. During the winter of 1795, in the span of just three days more than 1,200 immigrant sleighs left Albany on what had been the King's Highway. It would still be "Kings Road" to local folks, but to the wider world it became the Great Genesee Road. The woodland lane was overwhelmed with traffic.

In the twenty-first century, less than a mile north of Kings Road and roughly parallel, NY State Route 5—Central Avenue—belongs to a world apart from the pine bush: a swarming corridor of motels, car dealers, convenience stores, nail shops. But this was once the *new* old road between Albany and Schenectady. It was conceived and created "from scratch" by a cadre of pioneering city planners, surveyors, and financiers.

After the war the new state government—struggling to get organized, facing huge wartime debts, and a public outcry for better roads—passed a series of laws to improve transportation. Lotteries were set up to raise money. It wasn't enough. Eventually the state turned to private entrepreneurs, granting charters for turnpike companies to build, maintain, and operate pay-as-you-go roads, a privatized version of toll roads known in Europe for centuries.

The fourteen-mile-long Albany–Schenectady road was one of the earliest turnpikes chartered in New York. It was proposed in 1797, but financial backers encountered all sorts of organizational problems delaying surveys and construction for several years. The surveyor eventually hired was John Randel, a protégé of State Surveyor General Simeon De Witt. Randel laid out an American "Roman Road," an arrow-straight link between the villages of Albany (population a little more than 5,000) and Schenectady (2,500).

Randel's road is now the Capitol District's Central Avenue—diverted from the start of NY Route 5 on Washington Avenue. After finishing this job John Randel would spend years surveying Manhattan Island for the grid of streets and avenues that multiplied New York City. The Albany–Schenectady Turnpike roadbed was paved in cobblestones with smoother channels spaced at the width of standard wagon axles. It immediately became one of the most heavily traveled roads in the state, sprouting more than two dozen taverns. In time, Central Avenue has become a continuous, fourteen-mile commercial strip.

One fragment of the past has survived the raging development. About four miles from downtown Albany, near an intersection with Lockrow Boulevard, a dirt lane leads back to remnants of Grounds Farm, the area's last agricultural holdout. In the mid-1800s the Grounds family farm covered a large area on both sides of the turnpike, supplying produce to Albany markets. The crops have been gone for many years, but a narrow band of idle fields is still in family ownership, hemmed between housing tracts. Greenhouses and irrigation pipes are crumbling. A farm pond hidden in trees once did double-duty in winter, providing ice for area kitchens. Wistful plans to still find someone to plow the back field may not happen.

As Central Avenue approaches Schenectady, it merges with an extension of Kings Road called Albany Street, changing names again to become State Street, making the original descent to the Mohawk River. A traveler on horseback in 1744, Dr. Alexander Hamilton, described the scene in his journal: "you ride over a plain, level, sandy road till, coming out of the covert of the woods, all at once the village strikes surprisingly your eye, which I can compare to nothing but the curtain rising in a play and displaying a beautiful scene."

Where State Street meets Ferry Street, the old road entered the southeast gate of a palisade enclosing a Dutch settlement established in 1661, a few years before England took over New Netherland. As in Albany, sadly no Dutch-period buildings survive. A French-led raid in 1690 easily penetrated the stockade, burned virtually the entire village to the ground, and massacred most of its residents. Rebuilding began within a few years, inside a larger palisade. A fire in 1819 destroyed some commercial buildings. This and the opening of the Erie Canal, passing half a mile away to the east, shifted commerce away from the old neighborhood, leaving it to steep in the past.

A self-guided walking tour explores the street grid of the Stockade Historic District, a charming neighborhood of Colonial, Georgian, Federal, Greek Revival, and Victorian homes. The National Park Service calls it "the highest concentration of historic period homes in the country"; more than three dozen predate the Revolution. In the middle of the district, St. George Church was built during the French and Indian War, when enough English speakers had moved into the little Dutch village to call for services held in their own language. A series of plaques marks the outline of palisade walls.

For centuries, from Schenectady's riverbank, canoes and bateaux took Native Americans, European traders, missionaries, and military expeditions across and up the Mohawk River. The first flat-bottomed ferry started carrying wagons and livestock from the foot of Ferry Street in 1725. The first bridge was crossed in 1808 (see frontispiece), an event of enormous significance accelerating settlement of the Mohawk Valley and Western New York. It extended the new Albany–Schenectady Turnpike on up the valley as the Mohawk Turnpike, following the route of the ancient trail along

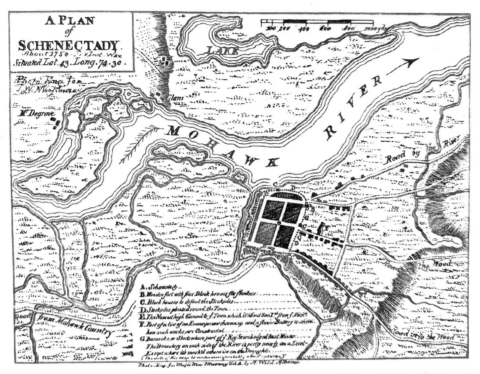

In 1750, most of the Schenectady settlement was still contained within stockade walls, though some dared to begin building along entering roads. French and Native American raids were a constant threat. "Glans," shown here on the river's north bank, indicates the homestead of Alexander Lindsay Glen at the start of the road beginning to take pioneer settlers into Mohawk country. The "Road into the Wood," at bottom-right, is the Kings Road from Albany. In 1744, Dr. Alexander Hamilton described "coming out of the covert of the woods, all att once the village strikes surprisingly your eye, which I can compare to nothing but the curtain rising in a play and displaying a beautiful scene." *Map courtesy of the Schenectady Public Library.*

the river's north bank. Trails ran along both sides of the river to native villages. Geography persuaded traders and pioneer settlers to choose the north path for a first road.

Near where Route 5 now crosses the river, remains of stone abutments at the end of Schenectady's Washington Street, and directly across at Scotia, stamp the imprint of the old 1808 bridge (see frontispiece). One central, stone pier lingered for many years on the tip of Hog Island (now called Isle of the Cayugas) before finally crumbling away long after the bridge itself was gone.

2

The Shifting Mohawk Frontier

Both the old ferry and the bridge (and presumably canoes) crossing the Mohawk River arrived on the north bank roughly where today's Schonowee Avenue dead-ends, in Scotia. Near here, Alexander Lindsay Glen built the first settler-house north of the Mohawk River in 1658. He was a wealthy Scottish émigré who first fled religious persecution to the Netherlands, then moved on to New Netherland as an official of the Dutch West India Company. A few years before the settlement at Schenectady, Glen negotiated a purchase of Mohawk cornfields across the river, later arranging a Dutch patent.

This would be the freewheeling way land was taken in these early years: a "purchase" or trading agreement made with indigenous residents, followed by a patent or land grant from distant Dutch or English overlords. When Richard Nicolls became the first governor of the Province of New York, he issued a proclamation: "The Governour gives liberty to Planters to find out and buy lands from the Indians where it pleaseth best the Planters. . . . Every man who desires to trade for ffurrs at his request hath liberty so to doe." Native residents were baffled by the European concept of land ownership. The *use* of land might be agreed upon, but to *own* land made no sense. However, if someone wanted to give a Mohawk goods for something he didn't own, why not? The scope and details of transactions were typically infected with corruption and/or deception and, frequently, rum—leading to trouble down the road. But in Glen's case he managed to stay on good terms with his Mohawk neighbors and even with the French. His farm was spared when Schenectady was sacked; in fact, French officers breakfasted at Glen's house the morning after the massacre.

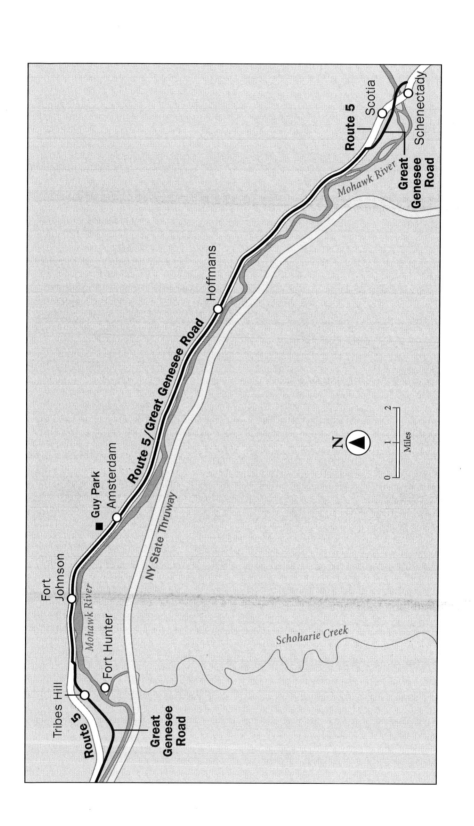

Built along the river, Glen's stone house—named *Scotia* after his native home-land—eventually succumbed to spring floods. But its stone was reassembled by his son Johannes into a more substantial house on the same site in 1713. That house sur-vives more than three centuries later, in a wing of a modern hotel, the Glen-Sanders Mansion, overlooking the river (and the Western Gateway Bridge) where Schonowee Avenue obligingly changes its name to Glen Avenue. The embedded Glen house is the closest we have to a survivor of the Dutch colony in the Mohawk Valley.

A grandson, Abraham Glen, built his own house just up the hill in the early 1730s, now located in Scotia's Collins Park. Although two generations removed from Hol-lander beginnings, it is a remarkable, two-and-a-half-story, Dutch-vernacular farm-house with steep-pitched rooflines and long, graceful dormers. Today it serves as part of a local branch of the Schenectady County Public Library. Furniture and household artifacts from the Glen family were sent down to Colonial Williamsburg in the 1960s and are scattered through that Virginia restoration.

Running through an old Scotia neighborhood, Glen Avenue merges into NY 5 at the edge of the village. Beyond Scotia's commercial periphery, wooded gullies and cornfields rimming the river bring a lingering sense of frontier after the clamor of the Capital Dis-trict's Central Avenue. Through the end of the seventeenth century and well into the eighteenth, this was the path into wilderness, the trembling edge of white civilization.

Captain Johannes Glen reassembled this house from the stone ruins of his father's 1658 pio-neer home on the Mohawk River (*left photo*). Glen's 1713 house is now embedded in one wing of a modern, Scotia hotel: the Glen Sanders Mansion—a striking example of adaptive reuse in historic preservation. *Left photo: Library of Congress. Right photo: Contemporary photograph courtesy of the Glen Sanders Mansion.*

The first half-dozen miles from the river-crossing were widened from footpath to cart road by 1674, the year England took final control of the Dutch colony. A few years later the English government sent an agent to investigate the "Five Nations of the Iroquois League," an entity still relatively unknown to the crown. A gentleman named Wentworth Greenhalgh set out with a guide on the King's Highway in May 1677, passing the new settlement of Schenectady and the house of Alexander Glen across the Mohawk, and on up the Iroquois Trail where there were no more European settlers. The trip took two months. He visited at least four Mohawk villages, forded the river, and continued to villages of the Oneida, Onondaga, Cayuga, and Seneca. His report focused on the location and size of each village, whether it was protected by stockade, and how many "fighting men" each nation possessed. This was not an exploration of native culture.

Greenhalgh and his companion were probably the first people to ride the Iroquois Trail on horseback. When they reached their end destination, the principal Seneca village of Canagora (today's Ganondagan historic site near Canandaigua), the villagers were fascinated to see a person carried on the back of an animal: "ye Indyans were very desirous to see us ride our horses, wch wee did: they made great feasts and dancing" and went on to give the travelers their pick of Canagora's maidens.

Modern Route 5 starts out from Scotia as a broad, four-lane thoroughfare obliterating all marks of history. The Genesee Road (and Iroquois Trail) hides under Route 5 like a mischievous old spirit, poking-out now and then to show a bit of the past, as it does a couple of miles from Scotia. An intersection with Vley Road begins a short, parallel snippet of the older, narrow road, skirting along stone fences past old farmhouses and barns. *Vley* is the Dutch word for valley. The old spirit–road will keep taking diversions like this for the next hundred miles.

At a point where the snaking river nearly touches Route 5, the road passes a stately brick home once an inn built in 1792 by Josias Swart, a descendant of one Schenectady's founders and the valley's most prominent families. Close by, partly hidden but with a historical marker, another house started out as one of the first inns past Schenectady: Vedder Tavern. Albert Vedder was a teenager living within the Schenectady stockade when it was destroyed in the 1690 raid. He was one of twenty-seven prisoners taken to Quebec. He later returned, married a granddaughter of Alexander Lindsay

Glen, and moved here to farm along the river, taking-in an occasional traveler. A tiny, Vedder family burying ground is hidden near the river.

In another three miles, before the hamlet of Cranesville, the old road breaks away from Route 5 as Riverview Drive, passing a nineteenth-century manor house backed by a cluster of magnificent barns. They testify to the expansive farms that flourished in rich valley soil, the soil that beckoned Yankees tired of growing New England stones. Riverview Drive leads to the pretty Cranesville Reformed Church and its large cemetery alongside Evas Kill. The first grist mill west of Schenectady was built on the kill sometime before 1730. The appearance of a mill marked a tipping point when there were enough farmers hauling grain to a distant mill to make a local facility commercially viable. The mill spawned the biggest little settlement on this part of the road for years. Here the Mohawk Turnpike put its first tollgate. Today Cranesville, in the shadow of its neighbor Amsterdam, has about the same number of residents it had two hundred years ago.

Evas Kill recalls the story of Eva Van Alstyne. She was crossing this creek on her way to Schenectady in 1755 when she was attacked and scalped, and survived, to see her name given to the creek.

Beyond the church, the bed of the old road is lost until it reappears parallel to Route 5 approaching the city of Amsterdam as Chapman Street, soon changing names to Main Street. The name Amsterdam suggests a major early Dutch settlement. It started out as Veddersburgh, a couple of mills on Chuctanunda Creek built by Albert Vedder. But rough terrain and contested land claims stifled growth. Despite the sanguine name change, the place remained a modest depot for nearby farms until the Erie Canal came along, changing everything. Suddenly mills sprang up along the steep descent of the creek, tapping the power from a three-hundred-foot drop in three miles, bolstered by an uphill impoundment. Among the many products coming out of Amsterdam factories, carpets came to define the city: Sanford-Bigelow and Mohawk brand carpets.

Pressures leading to the decline of northern factory towns in the mid-twentieth century—mainly competition from southern mills—hit Amsterdam hard. Today Main Street passes through a city still struggling to come back to life. From its own website, a too-familiar tale: "In an attempt to draw people and business back to Amsterdam, the City and State began a program of urban renewal and arterial roadway construction, destroying much of the original fabric of downtown. Now, not only is there less to go downtown for, it's harder to get there. Once again, Amsterdam is somewhere to be bypassed on the way to somewhere else."

The words "once again" recall the eighteenth century, when settlers coming up the road had their eyes on land farther up the valley and beyond.

Long before Amsterdam had any European settlers, it was the end of a trail between the St. Lawrence and Mohawk Valleys used by hunters and raiding war parties. In the fall of 1666 an expedition of 1,300 French-Canadian soldiers and Algonquin allies traveled from Quebec down Lakes Champlain and St.-Sacrament (Lake George), reaching the river at this point to punish Mohawk villages for raids in Canada. It was the first large-scale military operation on the Iroquois Trail. Many would follow.

At the western edge of Amsterdam, pinched between railroad tracks and Erie Canal Lock No. 11, a stately mansion known as Guy Park somehow manages to make everything surrounding it look out of place. It is one of three surviving eighteenth-century houses built in this vicinity with connections to Sir William Johnson, British Superintendent for Colonial Indian Affairs. Johnson gave the land for this house to his daughter Polly and his nephew Guy Johnson as a wedding present. They built a frame house on the site in 1773. Within a year it was struck by lightning and burned down. They replaced it with what is now the core of this limestone Georgian manor house the following year, on the eve of the Revolution.

Guy Johnson was a British official and prominent Tory at the outset of the war. He and Polly spent less than a year in their second new house before the hostility of rebel neighbors sent them packing to Canada. On the way, Polly died in childbirth. The Continental Army billeted troops at the abandoned mansion during the war. Later the house became a favorite tavern on the turnpike, and more recently a museum, until it was severely damaged by flooding on the Mohawk River during Hurricane Irene in 2011. After ten years in limbo, the house began a long process of restoration as an environmental education facility and offices for the Erie Canal Corporation.

In two more miles Route 5 arrives at a house William Johnson built for himself, seventeen years before Guy Park. The difference between these two houses reveals how much life changed in this part of the valley over those years, from perilous frontier to Georgian gentility. Johnson's fortified home is a simple, austere, stone square with gunports perforating first-story walls in place of windows (added later). It dates from 1749, when raids from French Canada had been going on for more than

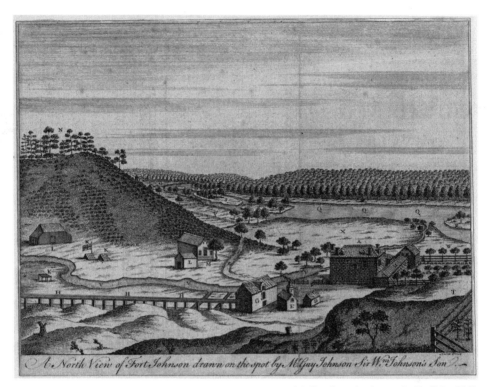

A North View of Fort Johnson drawn on the spot by Mr Guy Johnson Sir Wm Johnson's Son

William Johnson built his limestone house on the road following the Iroquois Trail in 1749. The drawing by Guy Johnson (mislabeled as a son; he was a nephew), made some years later, shows a developing homestead with various outbuildings, fenced orchards, a sluice-fed mill— the beginnings of a huge, baronial estate on the north bank of the Mohawk. The stolid, almost windowless fort/house hosted many councils between Johnson as British superintendent of Indian affairs and Iroquois sachems (represented by two tents). The house opened as a public museum in 1906. Instead of a lane clipping the toe of the nearby hill and circling behind the house, Route 5 now hugs the river. *New York Public Library.*

eighty years, leading up to renewed war between Britain and France in Europe and the colonies.

"Fort Johnson" became a prosperous trading post and homestead surrounded by farm fields, orchards, many barns, a granary, a chapel, and a long sluiceway powering a mill. Haudenosaunee sachems and warriors frequently gathered here for councils with Sir William. French raiders stayed away; the house's gunports were never needed.

William Johnson (ca. 1715–1774)

"He Who Does Much." *Library of Congress.*

Complex, charismatic William Johnson was a dominant figure in the Mohawk Valley during much of the British colonial era. He was an Irishman working for the crown but perhaps feeling some measure of affinity for the Haudenosaunee relationship with English colonizers.

He came to the area as a twenty-three-year-old to manage property acquired by his uncle Peter Warren, an admiral in the British navy. Warren's grant lay south of the Mohawk River. His nephew saw more of the fur trade passing along the river's north bank, acquired his own farm there in 1739, and opened a trading post on the primitive road. Here he became a key player, cutting out (and angering) Albany merchants by dealing directly with buyers in New York (city). He learned the Haudenosaunee language and cultivated friendships with chiefs and warriors.

Johnson's relationship with the Iroquois, particularly the Mohawk, grew and deepened into contradictions historians have struggled with and disagreed on over centuries. He was their great friend, advocate, and defender. He also usurped much of their land and drew them into Britain's colonial conflict with France. When that ongoing war flared up in 1754, Johnson was given a commission as major general, with no military experience. He enlisted a large force of Iroquois to join in successful campaigns at Lake George (which he renamed from the French *Lac du Saint-Sacrament*) and Lake Ontario. The king rewarded him with knighthood and the title of baronet.

After the French war Johnson applied himself to building his landholdings into what resembled a feudal estate, eventually totaling about 170,000 acres. With William Penn, he was one of the largest private landowners in British America. He recruited Irish immigrants and purchased African slaves for a labor force. His base of operations, the scene of elaborate councils with Haudenosaunee sachems and warriors, shifted from Fort Johnson on the river road to Johnson Hall, built in 1766 in the interior.

Johnson produced three children with a common-law Palatine wife. After her death he raised a new family of eight children with Molly Brant, sister of Mohawk warrior-chief Thayendanegea, known as Joseph Brant. No one has been able to put a number on how many children Johnson fathered with how many other consorts, most of them Mohawk and probably including Molly's sisters. His children from both common-law marriages, white and native, benefited from his will.

At council fires held with the Haudenosaunee, Sir William sometimes dressed himself in the trappings of a Mohawk chief. Indeed, he'd been declared an honorary sachem and given the name Warraghiyagey: "He Who Does Much." A military hero, a baronet who hobnobbed with Indians, dressed in leather and feathers, by some accounts William Johnson was the biggest celebrity in British America after Benjamin Franklin. In 1774, at one of his Johnson Hall gatherings, he collapsed from a stroke and died—one year before the start of the next war. In that conflict most of the Iroquois League Nations allied with the British, largely due to Sir William's agency.

After Fort Johnson, while Route 5 swings away from the river, Mohawk Drive breaks off to the left, then soon bends to climb up Tribes Hill. At that bend, Mohawk Drive continues a lost piece of the old path from Fort Johnson, its imprint still discernable on satellite maps. Once the site of Native American encampments, Tribes Hill is now a tucked-away, wooded hamlet redolent of the past. Walls of the Tribes Hill post office are filled with old photographs. At the top of the hill on Stone Church Road, as if in a Mediterranean hill-town, fissures creep up the walls of an abandoned church.

Another church has been converted into Tribes Hill Heritage Center, a repository of Native American artifacts found in the immediate vicinity and collected from across the country. Local items are Mohawk, but the story told here reaches back past Iroquois culture to earlier occupation of this area by Algonquian people, including signs of an ancient village located by archeologists on this hill near the river.

The road slides back to the water by the towered manor known as Danascara Place. A one-and-a-half-story, brick Federal home built here in 1795 by Frederick Visscher grew over the years into this grand Victorian mansion. It replaces Visscher's earlier home destroyed by a Tory-led war party during the Revolution.

Visscher was a prominent opponent of Sir William Johnson's son John in the run-up to the Revolution. The two men organized locals into rebel and Loyalist factions, taunting each other until Johnson was forced to flee to Canada. From there he led periodic British raids into the valley, most famously in 1780 when a party of five hundred Tories and Mohawk warriors took particular aim at the Visscher homestead. The house was torched, Frederick Visscher was scalped, his throat slit, and left for dead. However, he wore a neck scarf with red lining that apparently looked, to his attacker, like a rush of blood. He was not dead. He crawled from the burning house, recovered, wore a metal plate on his head in public, and lived to build a new house.

The next river town, Fonda, sits on a wide river bend. As Route 5 leaves the village it comes to the Saint Kateri National Historic Shrine. In the 1660s, Kateri Tekakwitha lived near here in the Mohawk village of Caughnawaga; archaeologists have studied the site on Hickory Hill Road, marking the imprints of twelve longhouses within a stockade. As a little girl she was the only member of her family to survive an epidemic of smallpox that left her facially scarred and partially blind. Tekakwitha—"she who bumps into things"—lived a short, shy, perilous life in the midst of turmoil as the French, Dutch, and English vied for control of the fur trade. After she converted to Christianity, too damaged for suitors and wedded to Jesus, a Jesuit priest recorded her story. She was canonized in 2012, the first Native American Catholic saint.

Several more miles upriver, hills close-in on both banks at one of the most dramatic spots along the Mohawk, known as The Noses. A native village on high ground above the path was called Tenontogere, "two noses." The ridgeline cleaved here by the river created difficult rapids for boat traffic before construction of the canal. A roadside sign marks the site of Spraker Tavern, where boatmen fortified themselves for a tough run.

In another few miles Route 5 enters the village of Palatine Bridge. Here the first bridge crossed the Mohawk above Schenectady, built in the same year Frederick Visscher built his new house. Palatine Bridge has the faded charm of a place left behind by changing times when the town of Canajoharie grew up across the river. On the north edge of the village a couple of historic markers commemorate "John Frey's house" and "Fort Frey." Neither is visible from the road, but both—dated 1808 and 1739, respectively—are still intact on a private lane leading to the river.

Hendrick Frey arrived here from Zurich, Switzerland, in 1689 and either "purchased" land or was simply allowed to build a log cabin trading post. He was probably the first white settler west of Scotia. We can only wonder what would cause a man to walk away from home in a Swiss canton, cross the ocean, journey up the Hudson, and trek deep into Iroquois country. The area became more dangerous as English–French competition for the Native American fur trade heated up. Frey's cabin was garrisoned with British troops during Queen Anne's War, 1702–1713. The log hut was replaced in 1739 with the sandstone house standing today, gunports on all sides. A big fireplace in the cellar allowed the family to shelter there through severe winters.

Hendrick had three grandsons. At the outbreak of the Revolution, Henry and Bernard joined the British army while John became a major fighting with the Continentals, rending the family as American families would be split again by war in the future.

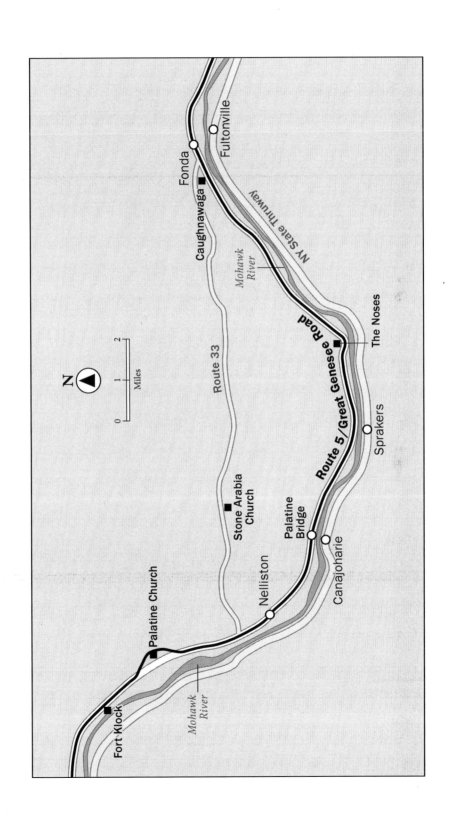

John eventually served as a delegate to the U.S. Constitutional Convention, and built the manor house in 1808 that stands next to the old family homestead/fort.

Palatine Bridge is the first of many recurrences of the name "Palatine" along the next twenty-five miles of Route 5. This was a part of the Mohawk Valley settled in early decades of the 1700s by refugees from the German territory of the Palatinate, a border area decimated by endless war with France. Desperate Palatines were aided by the British crown to settle in America, the first large group of German immigrants to arrive in North America. They came with the caveat that they pay for resettlement by providing the Royal British Navy with pitch and tar from pine forests for caulking and sealing ships.

The first workcamps, in 1710, proved disastrous. Deep in the woods of Hudson Valley's Livingston Manor, unskilled and short of supplies, the Germans barely survived bitter winters with the help of Mahicans living in the Taghannick Hills. A rebellious faction fled west, where British Provincial Governor William Burnet promised them hundred-acre farms along the Iroquois Trail, still Mohawk country and territory claimed by France. In a letter to the British Council of Trade, Burnet wrote, "they will be . . . a barrier against the sudden incursions of the French, who made this their road when they last attacked and burn'd ye frontier town called Schenectady." Palatine families became pawns in the contest between Britain and France for by the fur trade and Native American land. In their new country the Germans suffered again through decades of war, while neither France nor England ended up the victor.

Johan Peter Wagner led one of those German families to clear land near what is now the hamlet of Nelliston. He built a log cabin that was replaced sometime around 1750 by the stone house overlooking a field above Route 5 today, near Wagners Hollow Road. It was built directly over a well, fortified with gun loopholes, and surrounded with a stockade of logs that left archaeological traces in the soil. At that time the road passed close to the house.

Johan's precautions were rewarded. His house and family weathered waves of French and native hostilities. His son became a colonel in the Continental Army of the Revolution, fought in the nearby Battle of Oriskany, survived more waves of British raids, and raised a family of twelve children in the little stone "fort" seen today with a wooden wing.

The Wagners walked to church on what is now called Old Mill Road, turning off Route 5 before it crosses Caroga Creek. The ruins of a small stone bridge on this fragment of the Genesee Road probably date from days of the Mohawk Turnpike. Across the creek is the Palatine Evangelical Lutheran Church, constructed in 1770. The Wagners and the Nellis family helped build the church with stones gathered in the creekbed. Christian Nellis was also among the first Palatine settlers in 1723.

At the outbreak of Revolution, when the church was still new, members of the Nellis family took opposing sides. Henry Nellis went to Canada. When John Johnson's British raiding party came through here in 1780, pillaging and burning communities along the road, an officer reportedly stopped an Iroquois warrior from setting fire to the church. He had promised a friend, Henry Nellis, to protect it.

At the time the road was turnpiked, the Palatine church anchored the largest village in the area, with a mill on the creek, stores, many homes. Today there is one old house next door and a farm across the road. But the church is active and well-maintained. When it was restored for its centennial in 1870, workers found the thirteen-star American flag now hanging on display in the sanctuary.

A few miles past the hamlet of Nelliston, set back from the road, a small stone house with an old wooden wing was once home to the Wagner family (*left photo*). The Wagners and the Nellis family were part of an influx of German immigrants coming into the area in the early 1700s, when this was still a dangerous frontier. Just past "Fort Wagner," the ruins of a stone bridge once took the old road across a small creek. Across the creek is the Palatine Evangelical Lutheran church, built in 1770 (*right photo*). During the Revolution, when the church was still new, it narrowly avoided destruction during a British–Iroquois raid, saved by an English officer who had promised a friend back in Canada—a Tory Nellis—that he would protect the Palatine church. *Fort Wagner photo c. 1930 courtesy New York Public Library. Church photo by the author.*

Before reaching the village of St. Johnsville, Route 5 passes between crumbling stone walls as it approaches a sign for "Fort Klock." A colleague of the Wagners and Nellises, Johannes Klock built his limestone house on a steep slope directly above the river in 1750, adding a matching kitchen wing the following decade. Together they make an imposing, somber structure that was large enough to shelter many of his Palatine neighbors behind two-foot-thick walls, with few windows and many gunports, during frequent raids. Similar to the Wagner house, Fort Klock sits atop a spring. A nearby Klock farm-field was the site of a battle ending John Johnson's 1780 raid, one of the last major incursions of British troops into the Mohawk Valley.

Johannes Klock built this fortified house in 1750 as a trading post with Mohawk neighbors and a refuge for Palatine neighbors during decades of war. The Klock family lived here until their farm failed during the 1930s Great Depression. They moved into nearby St. Johnsville, and the empty home deteriorated until the 1950s, when a group of muzzle-loader-gun enthusiasts thought it might make a fitting clubhouse (Johannes served in the Tryon County militia). They leased the place from a Klock descendant and began replacing missing doors and windows, rotted floors, and roof. Public tours of Fort Klock started in 1961. It sits on a slope above the river, downhill from Route 5. *Photo by the author.*

The homestead stayed in the Klock family for two centuries, but it was abandoned in the 1930s and deteriorated until community historians started restoration. Since 1961 it has been open to the public, the centerpiece in a compound of restored outbuildings. One of these is a blacksmith shop alongside Route 5. It served the needs of the farm and travelers on the turnpike. When restoration began, blackened stone forges looked as if the shop had just closed, tethering rings still hanging from the walls.

Not far from Fort Klock, the flaming-yellow Nellis Tavern was similarly rescued from abandonment, in this case by the Palatine Settlement Society. Christian Nellis built his wood-framed farmhouse in 1747, just before Wagner and Klock rebuilt their wooden homes in stone. Nellis's interactions with local Mohawks aren't known. The house became a tavern and store. Its location tight against the road tells us Route 5 here follows exactly the imprint of the original road up the valley. Why was such a tempting tinderbox never put to the torch? Likely the same promise made to the Loyalist Henry Nellis in Canada saving the Palatine church.

Past St. Johnsville, Route 5 crosses the first major northern tributary of the Mohawk—East Canada Creek—flowing from the Adirondack Mountains. Before reaching the creek the original roadbed loops off as Old State Road, crossing the water on three stone arches of a narrow, brush-clogged, derelict bridge, perhaps another relic of the Mohawk Turnpike. Its survival through centuries of floods seems miraculous. It initiates one of the most evocative pieces of the old road, continuing along dressed-stone walls in front of wisteria-encrusted Beardslee Castle.

Architect and civil engineer John Beardslee built Mohawk Valley mills and bridges in the late eighteenth century, including first bridges over East and West Canada Creeks (in 1793) and the first span across the Mohawk River at Little Falls (1790). He settled on the road here by the creek in 1794, creating around him a community that, by the turn of the nineteenth century, included stores, taverns, a blacksmith shop, nail factory, cooperage, brewery, sawmill, and grist mill. It thrived and grew a population of about two thousand people until the Erie Canal diverted commerce south of the Mohawk River. What had become known as Beardslee Mills (or even Beardslee City) slowly died out and disappeared.

John's son Augustus built the limestone mansion behind today's stone walls and majestic locust trees around 1860, scaling it down from plans of Irish castles. In the late 1800s, *his* son built a small, hydroelectric facility to provide power for the castle and family farm, with a generator that eventually powered streetlights for the nearby village of St. Johnsville. That venture ultimately grew into the East Creek Electric Light

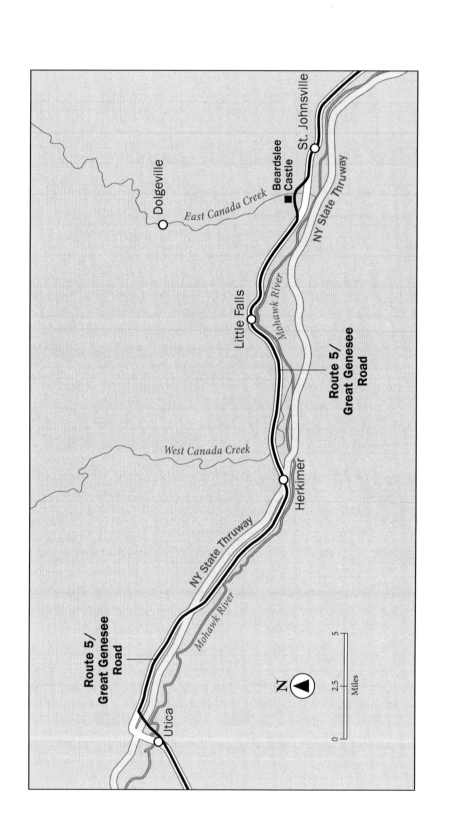

A narrow, abandoned stone bridge (*left photo*), perhaps a relic of turnpike days, lopes across East Canada Creek, the first major, northern tributary of the Mohawk River. The steel Route 5 bridge is visible in the distance through the trees. From the west end of the overgrown span, a short, dirt section of old road passes by Beardslee Castle (*right photo*) in a grove of locust trees. Architect and civil engineer John Beardslee designed many mills and bridges around the Mohawk Valley in the late 1700s. His son created this mansion in 1860 from scaled-down plans of Irish castles. Over the years it has suffered through two fires, multiple abandonments, restorations, and revivals as a restaurant. *Photos by the author.*

and Power Company, which (with a larger dam) became part of the Niagara Mohawk Power Corporation, which (with the involvement of a lot of lawyers) became part of one of the world's largest public utility conglomerates: National Grid. The remains of Niagara Mohawk's generating facility abut the pretty East Creek Reservoir a short distance above the bridge.

Close to the castle, a magnificent stone dairy barn built around 1850 has been re-born as a wedding event venue. The Beardslee Castle itself, after a succession of fires and years abandoned to storied ghosts, has found renewed life as a restaurant since 1941.

On its way to Little Falls the old road leaves Route 5 as Ashe Road, angles toward the river, then climbs high up onto another ridge squeezing the Mohawk from both sides. Where Ashe Road rejoins Route 5 they teeter on a slice of land between the notch cut by the river far below and a cavernous rock quarry to the north, a source of stone for Erie Canal locks. The falls at Little Falls are remnants of a Niagara-like cataract that once spilled glacial meltwater off this ridge.

Before Route 5 enters the little city of Little Falls, River Road turns off to hug the riverbank, the original route west. A middle section of River Road is closed to vehicles: a fine walk for a sense of the quieter days traveling by horse or foot along the water's edge. As the road bends up into the city it crouches under a New York Central Railroad bridge, which is in turn dwarfed by a thundering highway bridge headed over the river to the NY Thruway. River, road, railroad, expressway—four layers of the history of people on the move.

After the overheads, River Road crosses modern Route 5 to pass through Little Falls as Main Street. This is the course of the old road and the turnpike. Closer to the river, Mill Street more closely follows the line of the only major portage for canoes and bateaux on the Mohawk River between its headwaters and Schenectady. Mill Street is also the line of a primitive canal dug around the falls in 1795, powering Little Falls' first mills, forty years before the Erie. In 1805 the canal was upgraded with five locks stepping boats around the fifty-four-foot falls.

Massive nineteenth-century brick and stone factories present a jarring sight after coming through the valley's tattered, sleepy farmlands. The factories recall how water power turned Little Falls into New York State's first industrial center west of the Hudson, earlier than Amsterdam. But perhaps the city's deepest single mark in the history books came as an agricultural enterprise—America's center of cheese production. Jonathan Burrell settled a dairy farm nearby in 1801 and began making cheese. His dairy grew into the nation's largest cheese operation in the mid-1800s, drawing milk from farms up and down the valley and shipping far and wide on the Mohawk Turnpike and Erie Canal.

Outside Little Falls after Main Street rejoins the Route 5 arterial, the land eases down to West Canada Creek, the largest northern tributary of the Mohawk. Just before reaching the creek, the old way veers off to the right as Main Road, leading to stone abutments of a bridge that once crossed the creek north of today's Route 5 bridge. On the other side of the new bridge is the astonishing, ten-arched span of the Herkimer Trolley Bridge. It was constructed in 1902 for an electric, interurban line that ran from Albany to Utica. Since the trolleys stopped running in 1933, the stone bridge has waited with extraordinary endurance to someday, perhaps, become a spectacular pedestrian walkway.

Route 5 now dissolves into the commercial hinterlands of Herkimer. It could be the strip outside any small-town USA, but here its grim aspect overlays the site of one of the French and Indian War's deadliest raids. In the fall of 1757 a large force of French rangers and Algonquin warriors fell upon a large Palatine settlement tending fields spread over this ground. The French commander reported that his expedition "ravaged and burnt 60 houses of the Palatines, their barns and other out buildings as well as the Water Mill." Forty settlers were killed, 150 taken prisoner. Livestock killed or taken off numbered 3,000 cattle and hogs, 1,500 sheep, and 500 horses. Most of them were scheduled to be driven to market in Schenectady a few days later. The ground beneath today's parking lots is riddled with bones.

Most of the survivors had swum across the river to the protection of Fort Herkimer. They went back to their fields, rebuilt homes and barns, and restocked the pastures. Twenty years later during the Revolution, the Palatine farmers saw it happen all over again: the Mohawk war-chief Joseph Brant attacked the same settlement with a band of Haudenosaunee and Tories, burning-down scores of homes and barns, a few mills, and driving off or killing cattle. Because the settlers had been forewarned and fled to forts, only three died.

Route 5 passes through Herkimer as State Street, though the original route more closely approximates the parallel Albany Street, proceeding from the old bridge crossing. From Herkimer to Utica, scattered between roadside fruit stands and quaint motels, Route 5 shaves past the doorsteps of weather-beaten farmhouses. Their austere lines and "elbows to the road" tell us some were likely among the homesteads rebuilt again by indomitable Palatines, when the road beside them was narrow and little used. One of these houses stands out meticulously restored, the eighteenth-century home of a member of the Wohleben family, probably built shortly after the 1757 massacre.

Small, settler cemeteries also pass by at road's edge. With no church or fence, they have the improvised look of the frontier. But the NY Thruway roars "twenty-first century" nearby.

At Utica the Iroquois Trail and the original road forded a shoal in the Mohawk where the river bends north. This was a major intersection of the Iroquois east–west path with a north–south trail connecting the St. Lawrence watershed to the Susquehanna River and Chesapeake Bay. The British built a fort at this strategic spot in 1758, after the Herkimer tragedy, to guard the ford. Its site and the river ford lie underneath ramps of the NY Thruway, where the old route emerges as Genesee Street into the heart of downtown Utica. At this point, the early traveler's eye turned from the Mohawk Valley toward the valley of Western New York's great river, the Genesee.

THE TRAIL AND GEOLOGY

Imagine taking a walk along a seaside beach stretching from Albany to Buffalo—390 million years ago. The sea was a warm, shallow body of water covering most of western New York State for many millions of years. It was teeming with aquatic plants and animal life—mollusks, shark-like fish, coral reefs, brachiopods, all kinds of bottom-dwellers. The shells and bones of these creatures collected on the sea floor and were hardened and compressed over time into layers of limestone. The northern edge of that rock stratum—after the sea eventually drained away and ice sheets rearranged the terrain—is known to geologists as the Onondaga Escarpment.

To a remarkable degree, the route of the Iroquois Trail/Great Genesee Road shadows the waving arc of the Onondaga Escarpment from near the Hudson River almost to Lake Erie, as if the route still followed a beach on the ancient sea. After skirting Catskill highlands along the Mohawk River, the road strikes out cross-country, dancing back and forth across the limestone escarpment for three hundred miles. The layer of rock varies up to 150 feet thick, usually buried under soil but occasionally exposed in natural outcrops, at waterfalls (Chittenango, Seneca Falls, LeRoy), and at quarries (Caledonia).

Buildings made from the limestone quarries appear all along the old road—from Fort Johnson near Amsterdam, to the Gridley House in South Syracuse, to the Holland Land Office in Batavia—monuments of the Onondaga Escarpment. Ancient geology seemingly showed people a resourceful way across what is now New York State.

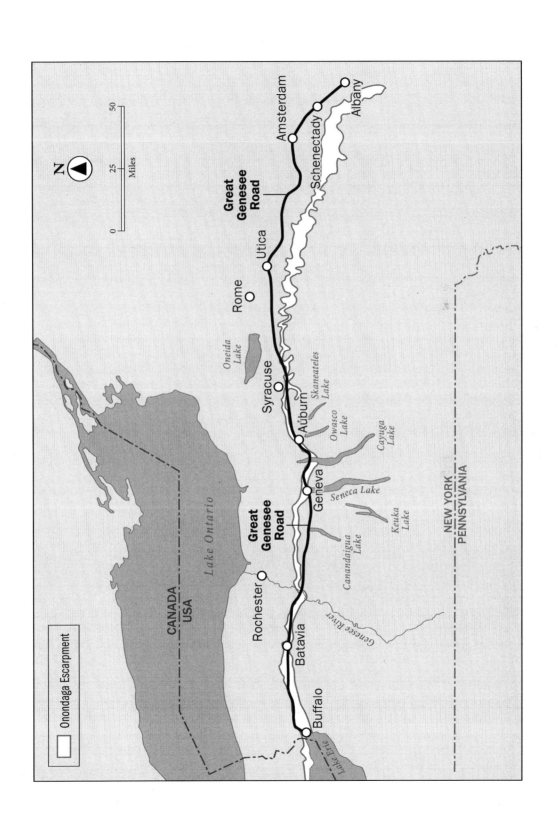

3

Haudenosaunee Heartland

The Mohawk Valley was disputed territory through most of the seventeenth and eighteenth centuries—occupied by Haudenosaunee; coveted by France; tentatively, incrementally taken over by Dutch, Germans, English, New Englanders, and others. Where the Iroquois Path crossed the river and left the valley to head due west, the road ended and the trail ahead was closed to any white settlement until after the Revolution. Only a few missionaries, fur traders, and adopted captives lived among the Haudenosaunee.

Following the French and Indian War, a decade of peace in the Mohawk Valley ended with the onset of the American Revolution. The raids now came down from *British* Canada, not French, and from British-allied Iroquois, not Canadian Algonquins. Mohawk Valley Loyalists John Johnson, Joseph Brant, John and Walter Butler, and others led mixed bands of Iroquois warriors, local Tories, and British rangers terrorizing rebel sympathizers, suspects, and innocents from German Flats to Tribes Hill. A particularly brutal attack on a settlement in Cherry Valley, south of the river, prompted General George Washington to take action. Rather than strike British military outposts in Canada, he determined to send a military force into the Iroquois heartland, more than five thousand soldiers under the command of Major General John Sullivan.

"The immediate objects," Washington wrote to Sullivan, "are the total destruction and devastation of [Iroquois] settlements and the capture of as many prisoners of every age and sex as possible. It will be essential to ruin their crops now in the ground and prevent their planting more . . . to lay waste all the settlements . . . that the country may not be merely overrun but destroyed."

Sullivan's troops entered the Haudenosaunee homeland from Pennsylvania in September 1779, quickly overwhelmed resistance, burned villages and crops along Seneca Lake, reached the Iroquois Trail near what is now Geneva, and proceeded west to the Genesee River. Journals kept during the campaign describe a heavily wooded countryside opening occasionally to large cornfields and orchards—summarily burned and girdled. Surprisingly few Iroquois were encountered, killed, or even seen; they melted into the forest, sometimes leaving food still cooking on campfires. Some hid in the woods. Many fled west to the protection of British Fort Niagara. Occasional villages escaped discovery.

When they reached the valley of the Genesee, soldiers were amazed to see vast meadows of grass growing ten feet high; thousands of open acres scattered with enormous, ancient oak trees. According to Haudenosaunee lore this was land cleared by another people long ago, "the old ones." With deep, alluvial soil, it was a chocolate-brown foretaste of the American Midwest.

The expedition retraced its route to Seneca and Cayuga Lakes, where contingents split up to sack more village sites and crops along the lakeshores on the way back to Pennsylvania. Colonel Peter Gansevoort led another group east through Onondaga territory to the Mohawk Valley and Albany, the first time a large group of white men passed along so much of the Iroquois Trail. Many resolved someday to return.

Sullivan's scorched-earth campaign dealt a devastating blow. The especially harsh, ensuing winter caused starvation and suffering. But the invasion didn't rid the land of the Haudenosaunee. Some stayed or returned after the soldiers left, and warriors resumed joining raids like Johnson's along the Mohawk in 1780.

While the Revolutionary War effectively ended with the surrender of Cornwallis in 1781, the door to Western New York remained shut to white settlers for several more years. First the peace negotiations with Great Britain dragged out. Then the new United States government and the new state of New York, not always in agreement, needed to hammer out treaties with the Iroquois Nations, who were also not always in agreement. Councils were held at Fort Stanwix in 1784 and 1788. The latter year marked the start of state-sanctioned settlement west of Utica, but it was a slow start into a roadless wilderness and a morass of disputes over land rights and ownership between the states of New York and Massachusetts; between the states and the new national government; between individual speculators, syndicates, squatters; between everybody and the Iroquois Nations; and even within the leadership of the Nations.

In 1790, six years after Hugh White brought his family to the edge of Oneida territory, William and James Wadsworth showed up at the Mohawk ford with an entourage
of three lumberjacks, a team of oxen pulling a cartload of supplies, and a black servant
named Jenny. The Wadsworth brothers were bound for the Genesee River Valley, 130
miles away, where their patrician older cousin Jeremiah had acquired, sight unseen, two
hundred thousand acres of Seneca land. Only a trickle of settlers had preceded them up
the Iroquois Trail. There had even been some previous, fitful efforts to start clearing a
road, but this trek would be by far the most ambitious. They hacked and slogged their
way through dense forest, treacherous bogs, across countless creeks and one big lake.

They cleared the road not just for their own passage but to make way for homesteaders on Jeremiah's real estate, and settlers would slowly come, eventually populating western New York's first agricultural empire, but for years the journey remained
daunting. "The road as far as Whitestown [Hugh White's growing settlement] has
been made passable for wagons," wrote a traveler in February of 1792, "but from that
to the Genesee River it was little better than an Indian path, just sufficiently opened
to allow a sled to pass."

Wadsworth had purchased land through a Connecticut syndicate headed by a couple of Massachusetts merchants, Oliver Phelps and Nathaniel Gorham, who took title
to the land from both the Seneca Nation and, improbably, the state of Massachusetts.
Understanding that conundrum requires going back to early days of the English colonies and royal charters. In 1628, as far as King James I was concerned, a land grant to
the Massachusetts Bay Colony extended from the Atlantic to the Pacific Ocean. When
Charles II took control of Dutch New Netherland in 1664, and renamed it after his son
the Duke of York, that province suddenly overlapped the Massachusetts charter. The
conflicting claims still held when British provinces became American states.

The two states hashed things out at a 1786 meeting in Hartford. Massachusetts
agreed to reduce its claim to include only land west of a line roughly running through
Seneca Lake. But, complicating matters further, that claim was determined not to be
for the land outright, but for the preemptive right of Massachusetts (superseding New
York) to *purchase* land from the Seneca Nation. It was this right that Phelps and Gorham bought from Massachusetts, for $1 million payable in three installments. They
went on to negotiate with the Seneca, purchasing clear title to more than two million
acres between Seneca Lake and the Genesee River, stretching from Lake Ontario south
to the Pennsylvania line. The price was $5,000 plus a promised annuity of $500 per year
"forever."

The state of New York kept control of land east of the preemption line of the Phelps–Gorham Purchase. Although the government in Washington asserted exclusive power to deal with the Iroquois Nations, under the Articles of Confederation the national government was weak. Governor Clinton and the New York legislature took matters into their own hands, making duplicitous treaties and purchases and setting up paper reservations of native land. They were eager to expand settlement west, including land owed to war veterans. During the war, Continental troops were promised land by the state in lieu of pay: typically 600 acres for privates; 1,200 for lieutenants; up to 5,500 for a major general. That, of course, would be Native American land.

Now veterans were coming up the Mohawk Valley to stake their claims. The abominable condition of the way west from Utica put pressure on the state government to do something about the so-called Great Genesee Road. In 1792, the legislature appointed commissioners to survey the route from the Mohawk to the Genesee Valley, codifying ad hoc efforts made by the Wadsworths and others to turn a Haudenosaunee trail into a road. But the state couldn't afford to do much more. As the first settlers got established along the route, they were enlisted to cut a wider swath of trees past their homesteads.

Little was done to the roadbed itself until the state passed legislation setting up lotteries for the improvement of roads, raising money to pull stumps and bridge creeks. In September of 1797 the road was good enough to carry the first stagecoach from the village of Utica to a small settlement at Geneva. The 110-mile trip took three days. It seemed as soon as the road was improved, it drew more traffic and quickly deteriorated. The same maintenance problems that plagued eastern parts of the Genesee Road—relying on homesteaders along the way to pitch in—were exacerbated in this sparsely settled country.

Enter the Seneca Road Company, chartered by the state in 1800 when lotteries had proved inadequate. Extending the function of the Albany–Schenectady and Mohawk Turnpikes, this private enterprise took control of the Genesee Road west of Utica, charged (optimistically) by the state with widening the roadbed to twenty-four feet and "covering it with gravel or broken stone 15 inches deep in the center." Gates were erected every ten miles and at key bridges, with rotating pikes swinging open when tolls were paid.

Turnpike tollgates didn't always have pikes or gates. They were often covered passageways where collectors could be sheltered from rain and snow. Toll-taker families lived in attached cottages. *Manlius Historical Society.*

A measure of the road company's progress can be taken from the journal of James Bemis, traveling four years after the charter was issued:

After being detained at Utica for upwards of seven weeks, I hired two wagons to take me to Canandaigua. They had proceeded about fifty rods, when one of them got mired to the hub! Good start! you will say. Well! We got out in about an hour and traveled eight miles the first day. Next morning, after taking a warm breakfast, I again "weighed anchor" and trudged in solitude along the muddy waste (for it is indeed solitary to have no company but swearing teamsters) till we reached Oneida village, an Indian settlement, where, about dark, both wagons got again mired to the hub! Zounds and alack! what a pickle we were in! . . . However, after lifting, grumbling, hallooing, and tugging three hours and a half, with the assistance of an Indian, we once more got "on land." It was not ten o'clock, and no tavern within our power to reach. Cold, fatigued and hungry, we were glad to get under shelter, and accordingly stopped at the first Indian hut we found, where there was no bed and no victuals, except a slice of rusty pork.

Nevertheless a steady flow of settlers now headed west, and farm produce even began to flow back to Albany, gradually making the Seneca Turnpike the most profitable (and longest) private road in the state, among hundreds chartered. The traffic included ox carts, Conestoga wagons, mail-carrying stagecoaches, massive freight wagons pulled by teams of horses or oxen, droves of livestock from cattle to geese, and many a solitary pedestrian with his bundle.

The later recollections of Samuel Ludlow Frey, growing up along the turnpike in its heyday, paint a vivid picture (he described the Mohawk pike at Palatine Bridge but the same could be seen all along the old road west):

> There was no railroad yet and the turnpike was very full of life, as all sorts of vehicles passed to and fro: Wagons with wheels six inches broad, drawn by six or eight—going down loaded with wheat or potash or ginseng, and returning with vast loads of flour and brandy and drugs, hardware, and a hundred other things. There were men and women on horseback, in chariot coaches, gigs and sulkies; there were great Droves of cattle and sheep and turkeys going off to the far off cities, and there were many emigrants from New England in canvas covered vans seeking new homes and fortunes in the far west. On many of these were painted in great black letters OHIO or GENESEE COUNTRY. Often these wagons traveled in trains and we could see them coming up the valley like ships under full sail. When we peeped inside the curtains we could see the children, or the mother or grandmother, perhaps, and the cat and all the furniture, the clock and the chest of drawers, for the wagon so large that there was quite a room inside.

Still, the turnpike remained a challenge. The "corduroy" of logs set crosswise over wet sections made a bone-rattling ride. Roadside farmers found their fenceposts yanked out to make levers for freeing stuck wheels. Two miles an hour was often good progress in spring and fall. Many chose to make the trip in winter on sleds, when creeks and mudholes (hopefully) froze and snow smoothed the way. An ox or horse could pull a load more easily on runners than on wheels. In the winter of 1822, on a wager, Theodore Faxton hitched a team of six horses to his sled-stagecoach in Utica and whisked a half-dozen gentlemen to Albany and back in a mere eighteen hours.

Another attempt to smooth the road came in the 1840s with a brief period of plank roads. There were now enough local sawmills to square logs used to cover wet sections of roadbeds. Why not cover them all? Durable hemlock was the wood of choice on the Seneca and especially the Mohawk Turnpike, where logs from hemlocks blanketing the Adirondacks' southern foothills floated directly down tributaries. Four-inch-thick planks were laid over oak rails called "sleepers." The ride was smoother and quicker, paid for with higher tolls. The surface was purported to last at least eight years, maintenance-free.

Investors rushed in. From the mid-1840s to early '50s, more than three thousand miles of wooden roads were built or chartered in New York State. But horses' hooves chewed up the planks. They soon started to rot and need replacing in only three or four years. Investors began bailing out, money for repairs dried up, and roads quickly deteriorated. The plank-road bubble burst in less than ten years. Hemlocks found another home in tanneries. The pattern for the Great Genesee Road seemed to be two steps forward, one step back.

4

Longest Bridge in the Western World

As it nears Utica, Route 5 (called here Herkimer Road) turns suburban. Amid newer homes a somber, brick mansion, partly masked in trees and vines, was once the home of General John G. Weaver, built in 1815 with a commanding view across farm fields to the Mohawk. Not far from here, around the intersection with Leland Avenue, the original road turned down to the ancient river ford.

In 1792, the state constructed a bridge roughly above the ford. Like virtually all the early wooden bridges across the Mohawk, it was soon carried off in a spring flood, and replaced five years later approximately where the Genesee Street bridge is today. Near the west end of *that* bridge a small park marks the site of Old Fort Schuyler, a block-house built by William Johnson in 1758 to guard the ford. The outpost was abandoned only two years later as the French and Indian War drew to a close. The park also marks the site where Moses Bagg constructed a log tavern in 1794 as the state began making improvements to the road. From the park, Baggs Square, Genesee Street proceeds into the heart of downtown Utica. (It is thought that the very earliest path of the road, and perhaps the Iroquois Trail, ran from the river roughly down what is now John Street, then Park Avenue, to where it joins Genesee Street at Oneida Square.)

Near Oneida Square, on Genesee, the Stanley Theater is a heroic survivor of the Urban Renewal that wiped out too much of Utica's legacy in the 1960s and '70s. The theater opened as an opulent, three-thousand-seat movie emporium in 1928, described as a Mexican-Baroque concoction with Iroquois references and Moorish twists up its pillars. Today it carries on as a multifaceted performing arts center. About

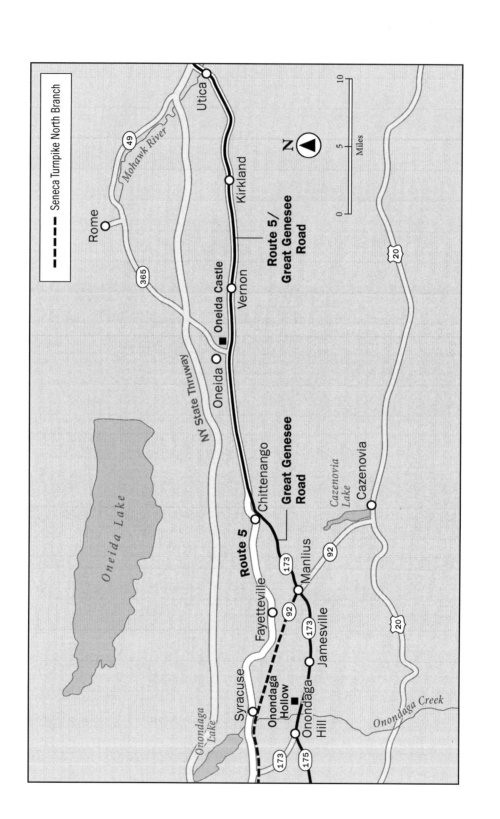

a block away, the modernist architect Phillip Johnson designed a centerpiece for the Munson-Williams-Proctor Art Institute, described as a bronze-clad, granite "floating cube" (it sits in a moat). The two buildings appeared barely thirty years apart, but to walk that block down Genesee Street is to take a psychedelic leap across the landscape of twentieth-century architecture.

The grand mansions lining Genesee Street as it leaves downtown Utica recall the city's glory days as a nineteenth-century manufacturing powerhouse. Inevitably those days waned in the twentieth century, when northern factories moved south, and inevitably the elegant homes today soon give way to strip malls. The four lanes of Route 5 bleed into parking lots, oil-change quick-stops, fast-food drive-ins, and so on. But outside city limits, road signs begin to call this "Seneca Turnpike."

By the time it reaches the almost-hamlet of Kirkland, the road has resumed an easy amble through farm fields. This was territory of the Oneida Nation, allies of rebel America in the Revolution. The first wave of immigrants moving beyond the Mohawk tended to pass through Oneida country on their way west to the Phelps–Gorham Purchase and the Genesee. Instead of observing a settled, rural landscape, a traveler coming out of Utica on the Seneca Turnpike in 1805 "saw not a single field which had not the stumps of the original forest yet remaining in it."

Settlement here remained relatively sparse for years. Where Route 5 crosses Oriskany Creek, a mill might have spawned a village, but this place is still rural. Its significance as a landmark comes from its name—Kirkland—attached to the entire surrounding township. Reverend Samuel Kirkland came to preach to the Oneidas as an idealistic young seminarian in 1764, carrying a personal good word from Sir William Johnson. French Catholic missionaries had lived among the Iroquois for more than a century; Kirkland was the first Protestant to become embedded in the native community. He lived with the Oneidas for fifty years, learned their language, became an honored friend, and—by his own account—learned more than he taught. His influence is credited with the Oneidas breaking from other Iroquois Nations to ally with American rebels in the Revolution.

All this might suggest Kirkland was a champion of the Haudenosaunee, but his agency was more complicated. When Oneida warriors fought with the Americans at the Battle of Oriskany, they fought against Senecas and Cayugas, effectively shattering the Iroquois Confederacy. After the war Kirkland played a key role in treaty negotiations, guided by his vision for native people and perhaps also by his own ambitions. He believed the future of Native Americans depended on adopting the white man's ways, giving up the life of roving hunters to become Christian farmers and tradespeople. Instead of defending native sovereignty, he worked with the state government to take Oneida land, including taking sizeable tracts for himself, some of which he used to establish a school where young Haudenosaunee and white men could study together. Alexander Hamilton signed on as a figurehead trustee of Kirkland's Hamilton–Oneida Academy in 1793. But few Oneidas ever attended. It became primarily a school for white settlers, rechartered in 1812 as Hamilton College.

The road beyond Kirkland is something of a cemetery alley. Beside a large, Federal-style home above Lairdsville, many headstones in a small plot are worn smooth, recalling how pioneer settlers might simply scrape initials or a name on a piece of slate. Stonecutters came later. The oldest legible stone here dates from 1810. A bit further on, the roadside Blackmer Cemetery may be older still, and in another few miles one corner of the larger Maple Grove Cemetery contains stones for the Marshall family dating back to 1806. The pilastered gable end of the Marshall homestead fronts the road just east of the next village, Vernon. The oldest part of this house was built in 1799, with additions accommodating operation as an inn during the early years of the turnpike.

Between Lairdsville and Vernon, Route 5 crosses the "Boundary line between the whites and Indians" established in a deed signed by William Johnson and chiefs and sachems of the Six Nations of the Confederacy in 1768. In the chiefs' words, the line was "fixed between the English & Us to ascertain & establish our Limitts and prevent those intrusions & encroachments of which we had so long & loudly complained & to put a stop to the many fraudulent advantages which had been so often taken of us in Land affairs . . . many uneasynesses & doubts have arisen amongst us which have given rise to an apprehension that the Line may not be strictly observed on the part of the English in which case matters may be worse than before . . . [but] Sir William Johnson has at length so far satisfied us."

There is no marker on Route 5, but a few miles south, two stones record the boundary line where it passed through what is now the campus of Hamilton College.

A short distance south of Vernon, a thirty-two-acre patch of land was, one hundred years ago, the last remnant of Oneida Reservation land. The precontact territory of the Oneida Nation had extended from the St. Lawrence to the Susquehanna River: more than six million acres. In the first official negotiations between the United States and the Haudenosaunee, Article 2 of the 1784 Treaty of Fort Stanwix seemed to reaffirm William Johnson's boundary line by pledging "The Oneida and Tuscarora nations shall be secured in the possession of the lands on which they are settled." Within forty years that promise was whittled down to thirty-two acres. Since then, through near-constant litigation with New York State and the federal government, the Oneidas have clawed back a diffuse patchwork of about eighteen thousand acres.

A gentle rise between bridges over Oriskany and Sconondoa Creeks marks the divide between watersheds of the Hudson and St. Lawrence Rivers. Sconondoa Creek parallels Route 5 from Vernon to where it approaches an intersection with NY Route 365 coming from the north. This is roughly the site of (and is still called) Oneida Castle, a principal village of the Oneida Nation in the mid-1700s. Route 5 is about to enter a quagmire of shopping malls, but here, around the corner on Route 365, is a quiet park under big trees, a place to imagine the native village. The same traveler who, in 1805, saw "stumps of the original forest" along the road from Utica, observed here suddenly the stump-free land of native cornfields.

The castle's war-chief Skenandoah was converted to Christianity by Samuel Kirkland. They became close friends and together facilitated the Oneida–American alliance during the war. The British retaliated with a raid destroying Oneida Castle, and later the Americans took away Oneida land. Skenandoah died in 1816 at a cabin on the turnpike where High Bridge Road now meets Route 5, just east of Route 365. He was reputedly 110 years old. He had watched nearly all his people leave for Canada. But still he asked to be buried alongside his old friend Samuel Kirkland.

After car dealerships and malls, the road west from Oneida opens to broad expanses of cropland. The soil takes on an arresting, reddish hue from underlying sandstone. On one windswept rise, a road sign identifies "Quality Hill Green. A company of horse artillery drilled here during the War of 1812." The Seneca Turnpike was the route of troops headed to the Niagara battlefront. Twenty-eight-year-old brigadier general Winfield Scott led an army of three thousand men along this road in 1814. Locals cheered them on, then cheered again the next year as weary columns trooped home.

There were no tolls collected, of course, for the military. Others who passed through the pikes free by law were those going to vote, to a doctor, a town meeting, a grist mill, blacksmith, jury service, church, or funeral. Freeloaders who tagged along behind funeral processions to beat the tolls were dubbed "deadbeats."

Before entering Chittenango, Route 5 bends to the right while Seneca Street, the old route, runs straight over a hill into the village. Names get a little confusing here. Seneca Street rejoins Route 5 briefly as they form Chittenango's main street, taking the name Genesee Street. At the far end of the village, Genesee Street turns right as Route 5 heads for Syracuse, while straight ahead is Brinkerhoff Hill Road—NY Route 173—the old track.

Leaving Chittenango, 173 quickly scales down to a narrow ribbon of macadam, pitching and winding with the contours of hilly terrain like a magnified footpath. It slowly gains elevation, undulating past a number of fine old homes and through hilltop fields that open a stunning panorama of twenty-mile-long Oneida Lake in its flat basin valley to the north. From this perspective it is easy to see Oneida as the receding remnant of a much larger, ancient lake of glacial meltwater geologists call Lake Iroquois.

About halfway between Chittenango and Manlius, near Palmer Road, Route 173 crosses the boundary line from Madison into Onondaga County. On this line, a few hundred feet north of the road, there is a small circle of trees within a fenced farm field. The trees conceal a cavity about sixty feet in diameter, thirty feet deep, once known as "Deep Spring," and before that, "*Te-ungh-sat-ayagh*," a famous watering hole on the Iroquois Trail. In the 1840s, an elderly Onondaga man recalled an incident that occurred at the spring when he was a young brave. He was traveling the path with several other men. Stopping at the spring, they happened on a half-dozen white soldiers resting by the water. They had left their firearms hidden near the trail. After a long moment of suspense, the soldiers tried to move on. They were killed and scalped. The old man opined that the Great Spirit never forgave him.

Deep Spring became a control point for surveyors marking boundaries of an initial Oneida reservation and the county line. Passing into Onondaga County, the road descends to the village of Manlius. Fires have erased some of the village's history, but on the west side, Seneca (Turnpike) Street passes a number of impressive buildings dating back to 1813. Smith Hall is one of a few crow-step-gabled, brick structures recalling days when the turnpike made this the region's first significant settlement and principal commercial center (Syracuse still being mostly a swamp). Christ Episcopal Church is Onondaga County's oldest, built in 1813. A plaque on the church wall notes the birth

This is what a turnpike could look like in the nineteenth century: a dirt road with what might be a passing lane looping off on a hill. In a few decades the roadside row of saplings will produce a nice canopy of shade. This view looks west down the Seneca Turnpike toward the village of Manlius in the distance. *Manlius Historical Society.*

of Manlius's first white child in 1794, the year the state first attempted to turn a cart path into a genuine road.

One casualty of fires in the village is the Manlius Cinema, damaged (in 1940) but a survivor. It opened on Seneca Street in 1918—a long, narrow, "shotgun-style" theater common in the early days of moving pictures. Admission back then was 8 cents. The place went through a bad patch in the late 1980s when the first few rows sat in a puddle from a leaky roof, but "the Manlius" lives on as one of the oldest continuously operating cinemas in New York.

About a mile south of the village, "Indian Hill" is the site of the Onondaga town visited by Wentworth Greenhalgh in 1677. He recorded "about 140 houses, nott fenced . . . situate upon a hill that is very large; the banke on each side extending itself att least two miles, all cleared land, whereon the corne is planted."

Two decades earlier, at this village in the bark cabin of an Onondaga woman, French Jesuit Fathers Joseph Chaumont and Claude Deblon held what is considered the first Catholic mass conducted in what became New York State. The event is celebrated in a tiny memorial park on Indian Hill Road. The Jesuits established a mission here, "St. John the Baptist," active for twenty-seven years. Shortly after the mission closed, the Onondaga village was burned to the ground during a French army raid.

Moving Villages

The Iroquois Trail linked the Haudenosaunee Nations, but it didn't necessarily pass from one village to the next. Unlike European towns, Iroquois villages moved around. In the early years of the confederacy they might move every twenty or thirty years: residents would simply find a promising new place, pack up, and go. The reason was often depletion of firewood and bark in the immediate environs. Women and children had the job of gathering wood. Eventually their foraging and lugging took them too far afield. Even hundred-foot longhouses were traditionally built to be temporary, regularly abandoned, and fade back into woods. Archaeologists struggle to find signs of habitation.

The time frame between relocations expanded in the seventeenth century when European tools like metal hatchets and other trading goods became available. By the mid-1700s villages were becoming more permanent, and some houses began to have chimneys and glass windows. But in another century they were all gone, and the trail was a road connecting towns of clapboards, brick, and stone.

Evocative stone walls border long, rolling stretches west of Manlius until the road dives into Onondaga Hollow, crossing the creek that flows north into Onondaga Lake. Most Syracusans have no idea that "The Hollow"—this dangling, neglected, south-end neighborhood—is where their city began. In 1792, this was the place where Asa Danforth and Comfort Tyler brought salt from the lake for a long haul to Albany markets on the Great Genesee Road.

Danforth and Tyler had driven livestock out the Iroquois Trail in 1788, meeting Asa's father at the ford across Onondaga Creek. He had come by bateau up the Mohawk and Seneca Rivers and Onondaga Lake with household and farming equipment. They were the first homesteaders west of Judge White's cabin (Utica). The only other white men in the area were a couple of traders causing trouble selling whiskey to local Onondagas. Observing Danforth begin to till the soil, the work of women, the Onondaga called him *Hatecolhotwas*, "the man who digs the ground."

Before they came, Danforth and Tyler doubtless knew about the Onondaga salt springs. Salt evaporated from naturally saline springs in marshes around Onondaga Lake had been traded for many years within the Haudenosaunee community, with the Dutch and then the English. It was never harvested by white men until Danforth

John Gridley ran a very successful tannery at Onondaga Hollow when he hired two stonemasons—Moses and Aaron Warner—to build this showpiece house on the Genesee Road near where it crossed Onondaga Creek. The emblem of The Masonic Brotherhood is carved in the entry-arch keystone, somewhat timeworn today but still readable. Gridley reportedly had it etched over his door as war with Britain flared up in nearby Niagara. A full-scale invasion seemed likely after Washington, DC, was sacked by British troops, and Gridley figured the Brits would surely be coming down the turnpike past his house. He hoped fellow Masons would see the emblem and pass by in brotherly peace. The troops never came, but the local sheriff sold the house out from under Gridley when his business went bankrupt. The house's thirteenth owners restored it from dilapidation in the 1960s. *Photo by the author.*

lugged a five-pail iron kettle up a trail from the road to the lake. He put his coat on his head, inverted the kettle like a helmet, and carried it through the woods. He and Comfort Tyler began boiling down salt from spring water, at first just for their own households. Ten years later they and six partners formed the Federal Company with thirty-two working kettles, the start of the historic Salina/Syracuse salt industry.

Near where Danforth and Tyler had cabins, a tanner named John Gridley hired a couple of stone masons in 1810 to build a house that still stands on the north side of Route 173 as it passes through The Hollow. It is one of the finest early nineteenth-century examples of limestone masonry in central New York.

From The Hollow, Route 173 ramps up a steep, wooded, eastern flank of Onondaga Hill. The aspect is not unlike a description in the 1805 journal of Yale College President Timothy Dwight:

> Rising out of Onondaga Hollow is a long and very steep hill. The road is constructed on the southern [sic] side of a precipice, in such a manner that, as you approach the top of the hill, you have a tremendous gulf on your left hand, at the bottom of which you hear the murmur of a brook fretting among the rocks as it is passing on toward the Onondaga Creek, which it joins in the Hollow. There is a kind of railing or fence, composed of logs secured with stakes or trees, which is all that prevents the passenger, and even the road itself, from falling to the bottom of the gulf. On the hill we found the embryo of a village.

As Route 173 nears the crest of the hill, a faint, dirt driveway leaves the south side of the road, perhaps a remnant of original switchbacks. It leads to a tiny burying ground encircled with stone walls and an iron fence. There are only two headstones, both for army captains in the War of 1812. One of them died while camped near here with his unit returning from the Niagara frontier. The other perished from smallpox on his way home to Rochester, released from a prisoner of war camp in Nova Scotia. The two probably never met but ended up lying side by side on this remote hilltop, having survived the battles but not the war.

At a crossroad in the community of Onondaga Hill, the path of the Genesee Road and Seneca Turnpike shifts from today's NY Route 173 to Route 175. A stocky, stone building at the intersection looks as out of place as a horse and wagon ambling into this busy junction. Easton Storehouse has *1823* inscribed in its gable. It has managed to adapt through two centuries from stagecoach stop to blacksmith shop, general store, advertising agency, clothing boutique, and dental office.

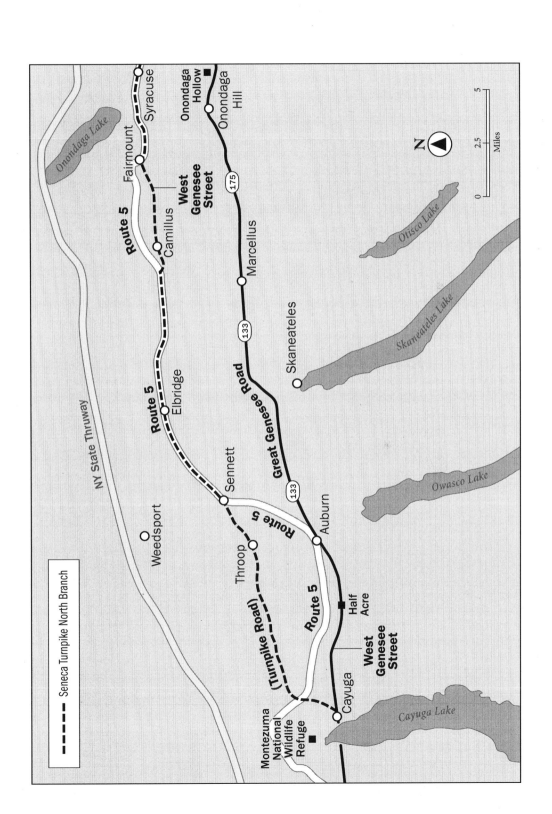

On a height of land west of Onondaga Hill the road passes below the imposing limestone General Hutchinson House, built shortly after the same masons made the Gridley House in The Hollow. Here they gave the gables bold, Dutch-style, stepped parapets. Orin Hutchinson was a brigadier general in the state militia. He grew up a bit further along the road in a clapboard farmhouse at the corner of Bussey Road, perhaps dreaming of someday becoming a general and building a castle on the hill. A wing was added to the back of the Hutchinson mansion in the 1960s for a restaurant.

Suburban trappings of Syracuse dissipate as the road leads to the pretty village of Marcellus on Nine-Mile Creek, the outlet of Otisco, easternmost of the Finger Lakes. This is the first of six crossings over outlets of Finger Lakes. Marcellus is among more than a dozen villages in the Finger Lakes area with names drawn from Greek and Roman antiquity. They were given to budding settlements in the early 1790s when the state's surveyor general, Simeon De Witt, mapped central New York. The names were chosen not by De Witt but by a clerk in his office, Robert Harpur, a scholar of classical literature. Timothy Dwight remarked on these village names when he traveled through the area. He found them "something singular, and I think ludicrous."

The old road, Main Street, climbs out of Marcellus in a series of switchbacks. One of these suddenly splits apart: signs point to "New Seneca Turnpike" and "Old Seneca Turnpike." The new spur was added when the village of Skaneateles developed on its namesake lake. At this point the old turnpike (now County Road 133) enters a beautiful stretch of rolling countryside dotted with handsome old farmhouses, a section of the old road that sometimes seems not to have changed much from early days. At Skaneateles Creek it dips into a shady hamlet where a narrow, shallow ford predated a road-company bridge.

Shortly after crossing into Cayuga County the road passes a white farmhouse once known as Nathan Leonard Inn. Leonard fought with the Minute Men at Concord and as a captain in the Continental Army. Twenty years later he moved his family to the wilds of Western New York, built a log cabin here on the Great Genesee Road, cleared a small farm, and in 1798, hung a shingle for his inn. Within a few years he replaced the log structure and continued lodging travelers on the new turnpike in this frame house. The sign is still in the attic of a descendant.

During the peak years of travel on the turnpike, the first three decades of the 1800s, there were inns typically every few miles. Today large, Federal-style houses, especially those at crossroads and those with two front doors (one for lodging, one for the taproom), were more than likely early inns. "There are as many inns as houses," wrote a traveler in 1822. One stands at the intersection of Seneca Turnpike with Chestnut Hill

Road beside a large cemetery. At the top of a knoll the oldest cemetery headstones include one dated 1806 for "Sally, daughter of Ebenezer and Submit Phelps, age 2 days." Ebenezer may have been a relative of Oliver Phelps, the land speculator key to opening Iroquois territory for settlement.

Old Seneca Turnpike (C. R. 133) picks up the name Franklin Street by the time it reaches the city of Auburn. Just as it abuts the Route 5 arterial that plows through the city, Franklin Street edges alongside Auburn's oldest church building (1815), now the Harriet Tubman Memorial AME Zion Church. The last home of the Underground Railroad heroine is part of a National Historical Park across town.

Franklin Street once fed into downtown Auburn's Genesee Street, the old route crossing the outlet of Owasco Lake. Auburn's remoteness in the early 1800s recommended it as the state's choice for a prison, located alongside the creek since 1816 and now the oldest in New York. The draconian "Auburn System" of incarceration became a model for prisons across the country. Inmates slept in solitary cells and spent their days working in strict silence wearing black-and-white striped uniforms. The first prison riot broke out in 1820, starting a two-century tradition of protests and insurrections. Today Auburn prisoners make New York State's license plates.

Separated since Chittenango, Route 5 and the path of the old Genesee Road rejoin at Auburn, passing through the city as Genesee Street. A view looking east up Genesee from the intersection with North Street, taken around the end of the nineteenth century, shows carriages sharing the road with a horse-drawn trolley. *Cayuga Museum of History and Art.*

At the edge of downtown, Fort Street turns off Genesee to the site of ancient Cayuga fortifications now on the grounds of Auburn Cemetery. Earthworks are still visible roaming between headstones. An obelisk at the top of the hill commemorates the life of Logan, one of the most revered Haudenosaunee sachems. On its base, a brief, powerful inscription comes from a speech in which the old man lamented the death of his entire family by white renegades, and the dispersal of his people: "Who is there to mourn for Logan?"

The old Genesee Road travels on through time. A few blocks from Fort Hill it passes the Greek Revival mansion of the Case family, prominent in nineteenth-century Auburn. Behind the house—now the Cayuga Museum of History and Art—a greenhouse was converted in the early 1920s into the Case Research Lab. Here Theodore Case and his partner, Lee De Forest, developed a technology for adding a "sound track" to moving picture film—a pattern of perforations running like a tiny railroad track beside the sequence of images. Fox Films formed a partnership with Case and used the new process in 1927 for what is generally considered the first feature film with synchronized music and sound effects: F. W. Murnau's classic *Sunrise*. The preserved lab is part of the Cayuga Museum.

A few miles west of Auburn on Route 5, the Finger Lakes Drive-In Theater is surrounded by farm fields as it was when it opened in 1947. It is the oldest continuously operated outdoor movie theater in New York, and among the oldest in the country. Cars can still hook onto speakers on posts. A new entrance bypasses this old driveway and ticket booth (*left photo*). A stone's throw up the road, an abandoned, overgrown, early nineteenth-century cottage (*right photo*) recalls days when the farm fields were first cleared of virgin forest. *Photos by the author.*

Leaving Auburn, separated by half a mile from busy Route 5, Genesee Road comes to a quiet four-corners called Half Acre, once a cluster of three inns and a stagecoach depot. Two of the inns survive as private homes. A journal from turnpike years describes more than a hundred draft horses stabled overnight behind just one of these inns, unhitched from freight wagons lining the road. Pens in surrounding fields were crowded with livestock on their way to eastern markets, a scene hard to picture in this sleepy crossroad today.

Near Half Acre the route of the Iroquois Trail tracked northwest to where Cayuga Lake funnels into the Seneca River. At that point canoes skirted the enormous marsh at the lake's northern end, today the Montezuma National Wildlife Refuge. In 1788, when this was still Haudenosaunee territory, two squatters arrived here from Pennsylvania: John Harris and his brother-in-law, James Bennett. Harris's father ran a ferry across the Susquehanna River at what became Harrisburg, Pennsylvania. John and James had the same idea for Cayuga Lake, ferrying occasional wayfarers.

The approach of the trail to the lake soon proved impractical, bogged down where it edged too close to marshland. The path was shifted south to eventually become the route of the Genesee Road, meeting the lake at what is now the village of Cayuga. Bennett took up residence on the opposite shore. Harris built a log tavern at the east ferry landing in 1790. This was all illegal. Treaties with the state and federal government had established a hundred-square-mile Cayuga reservation surrounding the northern end of the lake, and New York had not granted any right to operate a ferry.

A journal described the ferry in 1795 as "a rough boat, propelled sometimes by oars and sometimes by sail." Negotiating the lake was weather dependent: no ferry when it was too rough, no ferry when the appearance of ice became a hazard or when it was thick enough to walk and drive over. And no ferry when John Harris was busy pouring in the taproom. Still, on a good day by 1800 more than fifty teams crossed the lake. The ferry was already struggling to keep up with the flow of immigrants west.

When the state legislature began to get seriously involved in upgrading the Great Genesee Road, in the late 1790s, ferryman John Harris and a land agent, Charles Williamson, petitioned for a charter to build a toll bridge across Cayuga Lake, replacing the ferry. It was an audacious plan for the longest bridge in the western hemisphere. Williamson looked for investors in New York City. Aaron Burr, soon to be vice president, became a principal investor in the Cayuga Bridge Company.

The lake was (and still is) only six to ten feet deep at the crossing. About 225 supporting piers needed to be driven into the muddy bottom for the mile-long span. On scows or on the ice, horses powered pile drivers by walking in circles, winding up ropes that lifted trip hammers. Men worked hard too; company records noted "fever and ague being prevalent, a ration of half a pint of whiskey daily furnished to each man."

The bridge took a year and a half to build. It was wide enough for two wagons or coaches to pass each other on sawn planks that astonished travelers with a suddenly smooth ride after days of bouncing through ruts and chattering over corduroy. The tolls collected were scandalously high: "Every four-wheel pleasure carriage and horses, one dollar . . . every one horse cart and horse, 50 cents . . . every man and horse, 25 cents . . . every ox or cow, 6 cents." Burr and his notorious Manhattan Company were suspected of milking much of the profit. In a letter to Williamson he proposed over-capitalizing the company to provide a slush fund for speculating in real estate along the road. (Williamson declined.)

Eight years after it was finished the bridge broke up in heavy ice. It was rebuilt twice and used until the Erie Canal and finally the railroad syphoned off most of the traffic. In 1857, the Cayuga Long Bridge was abandoned and left to collapse. When the lake is calm, stubs of pilings can sometimes still be seen spiking up from the bottom. The eastern-end village of Cayuga, with old, wistful homes under big trees, has the air of a time warp. The first automobile, a White Steamer, drove up on Genesee Road in 1900, only to find the bridge out.

ROUTE 5 AND THE NORTH SPUR TURNPIKE

About five years after the Seneca Road Company turnpiked its part of the Great Genesee Road, a proposal was made to add a northern spur. The initiative came from James Geddes, a surveyor and early settler near the salt springs at Onondaga Lake. By 1804, the salt works had developed into a promising new industry, but it was strangled in cedar swamps around the lake's southern end. Geddes had an idea to drain and turn the area into a water-powered village linking the salt springs to the Seneca Turnpike. He proposed this to the state's surveyor general, Simeon De Witt.

Residents of the Onondaga Creek settlement at The Hollow, on the turnpike, ridi-culed and opposed the plan. De Witt settled the matter by packing-up his surveyor's spirit level and driving his gig out from Albany to investigate the site. He and Geddes got on well. He taught Geddes to use the spirit level, and the plan prevailed. Geddes made an official survey of the area including running a road north from the village of Manlius, the route of a proposed turnpike spur. In 1805 a mill was built where that road (now Syracuse's Genesee Street) crossed Onondaga Creek. Lots were laid out along the road. Henry Bogardus put up a tavern at the road's intersection with a path to the salt works, and Bogardus Corners became an embryo of the city of Syracuse (today the corner of Genesee and Salina). The northern branch of the Seneca Turnpike was chartered in 1806. Geddes sold twenty lots along it, and went on to use a spirit level in surveys for the Erie Canal.

The spur from Manlius later became NY 92, entering the city as Genesee Street. It picks up Route 5 designation at Clinton Square, where it crosses Erie Boulevard (the old Erie Canal) and then Onondaga Creek. West of the city, approaching Fairmount, modern Route 5 turns off while West Genesee continues into the suburban hamlet. At Fairmount's main intersection with Onondaga Road (R. 173), on the northwest corner, a house has gone through many uses (and accretions) since it began in 1808 as the turnpike spur's Brockway Tavern.

"Fair Mount" was the name of an estate James Geddes located here in 1798. His son George turned it into an innovative agricultural enterprise where Frederick Law Olmsted apprenticed as a young man. The last vestige of the estate, a stone carriage house, was torn down in 2014.

Genesee Street passes through the pretty village of Camillus, jogs south to cross Six Mile Creek, and rejoins modern Route 5, taking on the spliced name West Genesee Turnpike. It crosses Skaneateles Creek, outlet of its namesake lake, at a dramatic, looping curve in the channel, hence the village name Elbridge. An impressive streetscape here is celebrated by a historic district encompassing more than five dozen structures, many from the Federal–Greek Revival period.

In another four miles, Turnpike Road angles north off Route 5 next to an erstwhile blacksmith shop. This begins a delightful, winding, loping, dozen-mile ramble through a countryside of farms girdling tree-capped drumlins. Stately brick Federals appear occasionally on rises. The outlet of Owasco Lake is passed at the memorably named crossroad of Throop, with mill ruins in the creek hollow.

Turnpike Road crosses combined Routes 5 and 20 as they near Cayuga Lake and the huge Montezuma marsh. At this point the old turnpike spur split into two alternate routes. One proceeded directly west to the very northern tip of the lake, at the point where the Seneca River empties into and then immediately flows out of the lake. This piece of the turnpike, still called Turnpike Road, covers a distance of only about a mile as the crow flies, but it takes such a serpentine romp up and down and around hills that the mileage traveled seems two times longer. It's a rare, delightful snippet of a drivable footpath. It ends today at C-S Canal Lock 1 on the Seneca–Cayuga part of the Erie Canal system, worth a visit in itself.

The alternate end of the Seneca Turnpike Spur briefly jogged south on what is now Routes 5 and 20, then turned off as today's Cayuga Road to the village of Cayuga, the east end of the Cayuga Lake bridge.

The two routes of the spur may be partly explained by the break-up of the bridge at about the time the spur was being built. (The bridge was soon rebuilt.) Also, the experience of constructing a raised roadbed across the Syracuse swamp probably encouraged road engineers to plot a route through the lake's north-end marsh. In that case the road crossed the lake's Seneca River outlet and continued to Seneca Falls, connecting to the main turnpike, but that section disappeared in reconfigurations of the Seneca–Cayuga Canal.

5

The Fabled Genesee Country

Until 1800, Cayuga Lake could be seen as a de facto boundary of Western New York, a natural barrier extended by the lake's huge north-end marsh. The bridge and the Seneca Turnpike soon changed that. The bridge reached the west shore about a mile-and-a-half from the end of the lake. A lonely tollhouse rapidly grew a village of taverns, stores, legal offices handling land claims, and a large bakery producing hardtack for soldiers marching to the Niagara frontier. In the 1820s, steamboats landing at "Bridgeport" connected the nascent city of Ithaca, at the south end of the lake, with the turnpike stage line between Buffalo and Albany. Bridgeport became a transportation hub. The Underground Railroad passing through Auburn and Ithaca joined at Bridgeport on the road to Canada.

All this has vanished, leaving a quiet row of cottages and homes, Cayuga Lake State Park, and a lakeside burial ground where ferrymen Bennett and Harris repose. Lake Road Spur curls up the bank from the site of the tollhouse and heads west as East Bayard Street. A sign locates Potter Farm, where Nathaniel Potter opened an inn and blacksmith shop the year after the bridge was completed.

In about two miles the road reaches the Seneca River, connecting the two biggest Finger Lakes: Seneca and Cayuga. Native American paths ran along both sides of the river. Sullivan's army marched on the northern path, the way taken today by Routes 5 and 20 through Seneca Falls and Waterloo. But most of the earliest white travelers followed the Great Genesee Road along the south bank, what is now Bayard and then River Road.

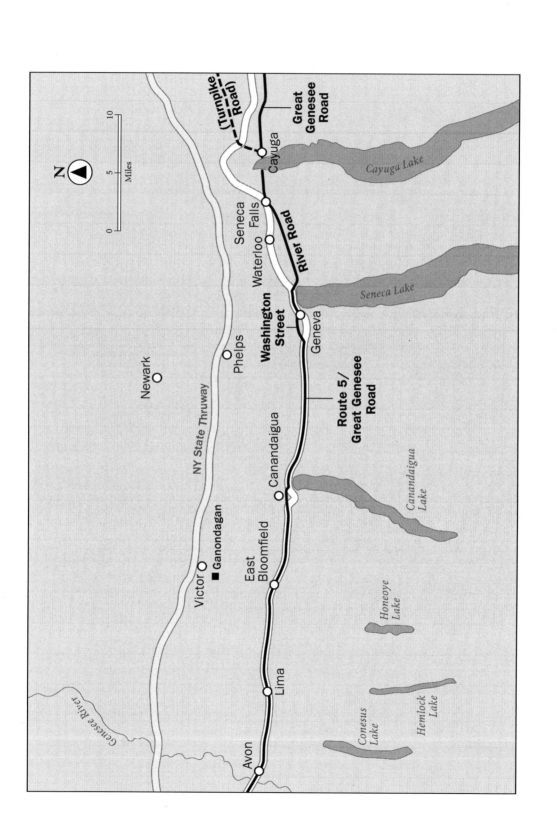

Where Bayard reaches the river and crosses a road to Ovid, remnants of a pioneer cemetery lie southwest of the intersection. It dates from the 1790s. Continuing a couple of blocks further west, Bayard passes through a quiet, commercial crossroad removed from the busy scene across the river. A row of two-story brick, step-gabled stores, frayed survivors from the 1820s, draws around the corner of Bayard and Bridge Streets. Across the intersection is the Franklin House, also brick with stepped gables, dating from the same decade. Once a fashionable hotel, it became a shabby rooming house. A street sign boldly proclaims this neighborhood the Sackett Business District, and indeed it was the original commercial center of Seneca Falls for many years.

A few blocks further along Bayard Street the elegant limestone mansion of Judge Gary V. Sackett is home now to Seneca County Head Start. Sackett began his legal career clerking in one of Bridgeport's law offices. From this grand home he ran a large farm along the river, setting aside one corner of property to develop his eponymous business district.

Names change from Bayard to River Road near the village of Waterloo. Here the road passes alongside Bear Cemetery, the neglected resting place of that village's first permanent white settler, Samuel Bear, deceased in 1807. He came in 1792 and built the area's first grist mill with help from Cayuga neighbors digging a raceway alongside the river. Dozens of water-powered mills would follow between Waterloo and Seneca Falls, tapping the forty-two-foot drop from Seneca to Cayuga Lake.

Across the river from Seneca Falls' busy main street, parts of the original commercial hub of the village survive at the intersection of Bayard and Bridge Streets. A corner-row of low, brick stores (*left photo*) dates from the 1820s, relatively unchanged. On an opposite corner, the once-fashionable Franklin House hotel (*right photo*) also survives, from the same decade but utterly changed into derelict apartments. *Photos by the author.*

Seneca Falls is justly famous for the 1848 Convention commemorated today by the Women's Rights National Historical Park. Seneca Falls is not known for its falls. In fact, there never was a distinct falls; mile-long rapids tumbled down the Seneca River until the construction of canal locks was completed in 1818. Boats were already carrying cargo between Seneca and Cayuga Lakes when digging the Erie Canal had barely begun.

A year before Harris and Bennett started their Cayuga ferry, Job Smith brought an ox across lake ice to the Seneca rapids to set up the region's first portage service. He constructed a cart out of hand-hewn logs, made wheels from slices of large trees, and began hauling the boats of traders on an ancient carry-path around the rapids.

Among Smith's first customers was a peculiar group of New England religious exiles searching for a site to settle a colony in the wilderness. They were the vanguard of migration by the Society of Universal Friends. The Society was led by one of the strangest figures in eighteenth-century New York: "The Public Universal Friend"—formerly known as Jemima Wilkinson—an androgynous, New Awakening preacher of free will, peace, love, sexual abstinence, abolition of slavery, and an early expression of feminism. The Friends moved on to settle along the west side of Seneca Lake, by far the largest white settlement in Western New York, but they were dogged by financial and legal squabbles, including the illegitimacy of their land claim.

A couple of years after Smith started his portage business, Lawrence Van Cleef built a log inn at the start of the carry and began ferrying travelers across the river when it was too high to ford. In 1802, a bridge came with the turnpike. Mills proliferated along both riverbanks. This part of the river is now called Van Cleef Lake, backed-up behind a set of double locks east of Seneca Falls village. When the Erie Canal Authority periodically drains the waterway for repairs, ghostly foundations of mills, houses, and bridge abutments briefly reappear in the river bottom.

Along conjoined Routes 5 and 20, the four miles between Seneca Falls and Waterloo have accumulated near-continuous commercial strip development. The village of Waterloo has roots dating back centuries to a Cayuga village called Shoiyase, "flowing water." Only a few years after the Sullivan campaign, the burnt-out clearing of Shoiyase became the site of a trading post run by Horatio Jones.

When he was sixteen years old, Jones joined a Pennsylvania militia shortly before it was ambushed by a Seneca war party. He was taken prisoner, adopted into a Seneca family, learned their language, married, and possibly had a child. At the end of the war, according to one account, he decided to return to white society and set off on the trail headed east, but one night of soul-searching by a campfire changed his mind and he walked back to his Haudenosaunee village.

White society, however, soon came to *him*, in the form of a twenty-two-year-old Englishman named John Jacob Astor. He had ventured into Iroquois country looking for someone to help him break into the fur trade. He met Jones, whose native connections helped start an enterprise that would eventually make Astor America's first multimillionaire. Jones also did well. He married a Schenectady woman who had also lived with an Iroquois family as a captive. They raised sixteen children on a three-thousand-acre farm along the Genesee River. His knowledge of the Haudenosaunee language and culture led President Washington to appoint him agent and interpreter in dealings with the Iroquois Confederacy, a job Jones held for nearly forty years through dozens of treaty councils.

River Road reaches Seneca Lake at the mouth of the lake's outlet. In mid-winter 1792, the journal of Charles Williamson records: "On the evening of the third day's journey from Whitestown, we were very agreeably surprised to find ourselves on the east side of Seneca Lake, which we found perfectly open and free from ice as in the month of June. . . . This after having passed from New York [City] over 360 miles of country completely frozen. . . . We then crossed the outlet of the lake and arrived at the settlement of Geneva." The great depth of Seneca kept and still keeps the lake open through virtually every winter.

Seneca Lake State Park rims this north end of the lake. A park path recalls the route of the old road from the mouth of the river along lake-shore beaches. The old way west left the lake on what today is Elizabeth Blackwell Street. At an intersection with Geneva's South Exchange Street, a sign marks the site of "the village's first log house, 1787, later known as Clark Jennings Tavern." It was one of three squatters' huts in this vicinity while regional treaty negotiations and land claims were still in flux.

From here the original roadbed climbed up the bluff ahead in a switchback partly preserved by Carter Alley. The alley dead-ends at the bottom of a steep gap amid elegant row houses lining Geneva's South Main Street. A stone walkway alongside an Elks Lodge mansion climbs up that last rise to the top of the bluff. Directly across a pretty village green—Pulteney Park—the Genesee Road continued on the line of present-day Washington Street.

This charming, brick-paved neighborhood of townhouses and stately homes along South Main Street, unique in the Finger Lakes, is the old center of Geneva, entirely distinct from the city's current downtown. At the corner of Washington Street, the Pulteney House Apartments dominate the park. The front section of this structure was built by Charles Williamson in 1796 as the Geneva Hotel, to accommodate and expedite early settlers headed west on the Great Genesee Road. A large, three-story porch has been added, but behind it and in a wing to the left, the hotel of old etchings is still there.

Williamson had to bring from Albany—over still-challenging roads and the Cayuga Lake sail-ferry—nearly everything needed to build, equip, and furnish a first-class hotel. He hired an English nobleman's butler as maître-d'. It must have been astonishing for travelers to encounter a lavishly appointed hotel perched on the bluff looking across Seneca Lake at seemingly boundless wilderness. The occasion of the hotel's grand opening coincided with the christening of Seneca Lake's first packet boat, the sloop *Alexander*, set to make regular runs the length of the lake between Geneva and Queen Catherine's Town (Montour Falls). The joint celebration drew a crowd of two thousand from the surrounding area, everyone reportedly amazed to see they had so many neighbors. The new hotel soon received the first passenger-mail wagon to travel the road west from Utica, a three-day trip if the Harris ferry wasn't delayed. Until then mail had been delivered on horseback.

The Geneva Hotel was one of the key stops for stagecoaches on the Old Genesee Road. Hemenway owned the place in 1832 when the building was already more than thirty-five years old, the first truly stylish hotel in western New York. Land agent Charles Williamson built it in 1796 to expedite the flow of settlers to Genesee Country. In its third century the hotel has added a massive portico and fourth floor, but as the Pulteney Apartments (*right photo*), the building still shows its provenance, sensitively preserved outside and in. *Left image: Geneva Historical Society. Right image: Photo by the author.*

Charles Williamson wrote, "the road from Fort Schuyler, on the Mohawk River, to Genesee, from being, in the month of June, 1797, little better than an Indian path, was so far improved that a stage started from Fort Schuyler on the 30th of September and arrived at the hotel in Geneva in the afternoon of the third day, with four passengers. This line of road having been established by law, not less than fifty families settled on it in the space of four months after it was opened."

Charles Williamson (1757–1808)

A diligent Scot. *New York Public Library.*

Charles Williamson was probably the single most important person in the evolution of the Great Genesee Road. He was an ambitious, diligent Scot with an interesting story. While in his early twenties, on the way to serve against the North American rebellion, his ship was captured by a French privateer and taken to Boston. Since he was still technically a noncombatant, instead of military prison he was put under house arrest with a family in Roxbury. There he fell ill, was nursed by a daughter in the household, the two fell in love, and after the war he took her back to Scotland.

Years later he fell in with a group of Scottish investors looking for someone to oversee land they had arranged to purchase in Western New York. Following the Revolution there was a scramble among wealthy Europeans to buy undeveloped land in America. The New York legislature reacted by implementing a ban on land ownership by "aliens." The Scottish speculators needed an accomplice who could acquire American citizenship—someone, for example, with an American wife. The group was led by Lord William Pulteney, one of the richest men in Britain. He had negotiated the purchase of 1,264,000 acres from Robert Morris, one of the richest men in America, who had recently bought most of the defaulted Phelps–Gorham Purchase. Charles Williamson became the titular head of the new Pulteney Purchase.

Ten years after his first trip to America, Williamson brought his young family on another miserable Atlantic crossing that almost killed his daughter. In the winter of 1792 he hired a guide, took a carriage to Whitesboro, and continued by sled on the track opened two years earlier by the Wadsworth brothers. In three days they crossed the eastern boundary of the Pulteney Purchase at Seneca Lake, moving on to the western boundary at the Genesee River. The land fired up an already fertile mind. Williamson erected log-hut sales offices in hamlets at Canandaigua and Geneva, lobbied the state for improvements to the road, and built a posh hotel overlooking Seneca Lake (with an English butler). It was the first in a chain of inns to lure settlers into the wilderness. He was a principal backer, along with Aaron Burr, of the Long Bridge across Cayuga Lake.

At the same time, Williamson personally supervised cutting a second road into Western New York from Pennsylvania, working with legendary guide Benjamin Patterson, a cousin of Daniel Boone. The southern route was meant to bring up plantation owners and slave labor.

Alas, the Pulteney Associates decided he was spending too much money and dismissed Williamson when New York lifted its restrictions on land ownership in 1800. He then became embroiled in his friend Aaron Burr's infamous scheme to establish a fiefdom in Louisiana (and maybe Mexico). He was trying to help Burr win British government support, but Britain was too busy with Napoleon Bonaparte.

Charles Williamson died of malaria on one last horrific crossing to England in 1808. His wife, Abigail, lived in Geneva for another sixteen years, watching a land office grow into a village.

Behind Geneva's Pulteney Apartments, the first block of Washington Street contains a row of old, brick storefronts hinting at days when this was Western New York's first commercial center. Across the street, in front of an eclectic, Greek Revival home, a historical sign identifies the "Site of Pulteney Land Office." The stone core of this building is thought to be the fifth location of land offices that shifted around the new settlement after 1792, this one operating from 1824 until the Pulteney Associates venture disbanded in 1858. With wings added later, it now houses a branch residence of the Elmira Psychiatric Center.

Nearby, on a side lane off Pulteney Park, a dark-green clapboard house is perhaps the oldest structure in Geneva. Recently restored with care, it is presumed to have housed workers—builders, cook, drayman—of the hotel around the corner. Directly across the lane a small building may have been their workshop.

A few blocks from Pulteney Park, Washington Street passes alongside one of the city's old cemeteries on the way to the city's edge, where the street runs into commercial development. Here the path of the Genesee Road is picked up by Routes 5 and 20. And here the boundary of the city is marked by the north–south line of Pre-Emption Road.

People living around this part of the Finger Lakes sometimes wonder about the name Pre-Emption Road, and may even do a little research, but they soon tend to

Located just off Geneva's Pulteney Park, this house looks like it was plucked from the edge of a New England village green. Workers hired to build the nearby Geneva Hotel came from New England, like most of the people traveling out the Genesee Road. Records are missing, but this was likely constructed as housing for the hotel's builders and first staff. As such, from the 1790s it may be the oldest frame house in Western New York. It has been quietly, respectfully restored as a private, duplex home—one of the delights of wandering around this charming Geneva neighborhood. *Photo by the author.*

throw up their hands. The tangle of land claims and treaties (outlined in chapter 3) took one more twist when a resurvey of the New York–Massachusetts Pre-Emption boundary shifted the line from the middle of Seneca Lake to what is now the western edge of Geneva. The land west of Pre-Emption Road came to be the Phelps–Gorham Purchase, later the Pulteney Purchase, more loosely called Genesee Country (although the Genesee River is still fifty miles away).

From here, alongside Routes 5 and 20, the land rolls gently in long fields of cabbage, corn, and beans. Chronicles of the Sullivan Campaign describe miles of this land as "old fields which had been cultivated at an earlier day but were overgrown with bushes and grass." Near the Seneca village of Kanadesaga (which they burned), they did find and girdle a large peach orchard. Two decades later, trees sprouted from old roots were producing fruit again, harvested by a white settler who sold one hundred bushels to a Geneva distillery.

Until a recent sad day of demolition, the patterned slates of a roadside barn roof recorded its date as 1813. A few miles west of Geneva the old roadbed breaks off Routes 5 and 20 on a short loop called Sand Hill Road. It passes a settler cemetery shrouded behind bushes, the oldest legible stone dated 1808.

A hamlet at the crossing of Flint Creek includes a one-time carriage factory powered by the creek. The first bridge here was one of the turnpike's earliest, in 1800. Before a slope descends to the small city of Canandaigua, near an intersection with Mumby Road there is another pioneer cemetery: Hopewell Burying Ground, oldest stone 1805.

At the eastern edge of Canandaigua the old route mercifully dodges Routes 5 and 20 strip development by following Lakeside Drive around the end of Canandaigua Lake. As it bends to head uphill into the city proper, the drive passes one of the old turnpike taverns, Colonial Inn, now Murphy's Law Irish Pub.

The original route through Canandaigua roughly ran up present South Main Street and turned onto West Avenue. Near their intersection, the First Congregational Church must have thrilled the little village when twin doors opened in 1799—a grand, brick outpost of Christianity in the wilderness. Only eleven years earlier, Phelps and Gorham had acquired their huge tract and opened one of the new nation's first land sales offices at a clearing thought to be where Canandaigua's cemetery on West Avenue is located today. At that clearing the Continental Army had torched the Seneca village of Kanandaiqua, described in General Sullivan's report as twenty-three "very elegant, mostly framed" longhouses made with hewn planks and masonry chimneys.

By the time the First Congregational Church opened, Canandaigua had a courthouse, a jail, an academy, and a weekly market. An elegant village had risen again from ashes. On the south side of West Avenue, Canandaigua's own pioneer cemetery holds the remains of Oliver Phelps, his wife, Mary, children, and grandchildren. His land speculation with Nathaniel Gorham didn't go well. In their first two years they were unable to lure enough settlers out the rough track of the Genesee Road to keep up with payments to Massachusetts. The syndicate defaulted, and "the Purchase" was snapped up by Robert Morris, renowned financier of the Revolution. Phelps went on to other speculative disasters. He spent his last years in Canandaigua trying to redeem his and Gorham's failed venture by helping struggling, mortgaged farms stay afloat. He ended up in debtor's prison, where he died.

West Avenue climbs from the village to reconnect with Routes 5 and 20 in rich, wide-open, gravelly loam farmland, the Genesee Country destination of so many weary, hopeful travelers. Occasionally where the undulating road rises, a handsome, nineteenth-century brick home looks out over prosperous fields, though the houses may now belong to more Canandaigua and Rochester commuters than working farm families.

East Bloomfield is the first rural community, a hamlet built around a generous public square set off in 1798. It has the aspect of a stretched-out New England village green, flanked by a couple of early churches. In 1808, village blacksmith Peter Holloway opened a turnpike inn still standing at one corner of the green. But dominating the square is a big, brick edifice built in 1838 as the East Bloomfield Academy, a coeducational boarding school established at a time when such gender-progressive institutions were rare. It operated until 1909, later becoming home to the village historical society. Behind it, signs memorialize an original burying ground moved to an opposite corner of the square.

So many villages along the old road were settled at clearings made by earlier residents. East Bloomfield is the approximate site of a Seneca village called Gandougarae and a Jesuit Mission of St. Michael. In 1669, the explorer René-Robert Cavelier, Sieur de La Salle, showed up at the village mission looking for directions to the Mississippi River. In Canada he had heard tales of a great river in the west that emptied to the sea, a possible trade route to China. This was La Salle's first foray as an explorer, and it didn't go well. He was hundreds of miles off the mark, the Seneca refused to serve as guides, he fell ill with fever, and after a month at Gandougarae, retreated to Canada. He eventually did find the Mississippi and build a string of French forts, but he ended his days lost in Texas and shot by one of his own men.

For years, early farmers in the Bloomfield area plowed up gun barrels, locks, and miscellaneous hardware identified as French-made. They were sometimes recycled to mend and make farming implements. Farms generally included small herds of livestock. One homesteader later bemoaned that, among many trials endured, "there were none more irritating than the destruction of sheep and swine by the wolves and bears. Often whole flocks of sheep would be slaughtered in the night by the wolves. Bears preyed upon the hogs that, from necessity, new settlers were obliged to let run in the woods for shack." The reminiscence went on about a man who "came pretty near

The East Bloomfield Academy was one of the largest school buildings of its time in this part of the state. It was also a pioneer: a coeducational boarding school in 1839. The academy operated for seventy years. The Bloomfield Historical Society has called the building home since 1970, gradually restoring its three floors of dormitory and school rooms and filling them with thousands of local artifacts. *Photo by the author.*

having a clinch with one [bear] while in the woods splitting rails. Stooping down to pick up his ax he turned around and found him self confronted by a bear standing on his hind legs, with fore paws extended to give him a hug. He declined the offer, struck the bear in the head with the ax, but making a glancing stroke, failed to penetrate the skull. The bear fled, bearing off the ax which was held by the wounded skin and flesh."

One of the first settlers on the Phelps–Gorham Purchase, Oliver Chapin, stopped at the Canandaigua land office in 1790 to purchase a three-hundred-acre homestead near what became East Bloomfield. He brought apple seedlings from Connecticut. Crossbreeding in his orchard led to a new cultivar—Northern Spy— Genesee Country agriculture's first celebrity crop, and still a favorite variety among Northeast apple afficionados. At some point someone in Bloomfield's active Underground Railroad named the new apple after a popular dime-store novel about a wily abolitionist operating in the South.

In a few more miles the tiny hamlet of West Bloomfield has saved a number of its first houses. Watrous Peck came out the Genesee Road from Connecticut before it was turnpiked. His 1803 Georgian-colonial-style homestead survives in great shape with its massive central chimney, original clapboards, and a domed, brick-lined pantry. Down the road one of the turnpike's early stagecoach inns, Johnson Tavern, ca. 1804, was built from bricks made onsite. Just west of the hamlet a turn-off on Factory Hollow Road leads to a piece of the old roadbed where it crossed Honeoye Creek, the outlet of Honeoye Lake. Here travelers passed a landmark: the first tributary of the Genesee River watershed. The bridge is long gone, leaving overgrown stone abutments. Across the creek, Dussett Lane returns the turnpike roadbed to Routes 5 and 20.

Sixteen miles west of Canandaigua the charming village of Lima replaces a Seneca village called Gondichiragou, "forks of the trail." At this point the east–west Iroquois Trail crossed a north–south path coming from Irondequoit Bay on Lake Ontario (now Route 15A). This intersection first appears in French fur-trader accounts from 1634. It became the site of a Jesuit mission in 1668. Artifacts of several palisaded, Seneca longhouse villages have turned up through the years in the backyards and farm fields around Lima. The first white settlers here were Paul Davison and Jonathan Gould, veterans of the Sullivan–Clinton expedition. They returned in 1788 to a site abandoned by the Iroquois but not destroyed during the campaign. (From Canandaigua west, the Continental Army left the main Iroquois Trail, tracking southwest to Conesus and Hemlock Lakes and reaching the Genesee River at what is now Geneseo, returning on the same route.)

Travelers on the Genesee Road found a succession of accommodations at this forks of the trail since the early 1790s, most recently at today's brick American Hotel, built around 1860 for the stagecoach trade. Lima (named after the Connecticut town of Old Lyme and similarly pronounced like the bean) became the commercial hub of Genesee Country in the early decades of the 1800s. More than a dozen houses listed on the National Historic Register line Main Steet, the oldest dating back to 1806. They testify to the prosperity quickly springing from the valley's rich farms. A center of academia in Western New York also took root here beginning with the Genesee Wesleyan Seminary in 1831, one of the nation's first coeducational academies, followed by Genesee

College twenty years later. The college's commanding, Greek Revival hall (now part of Elim Bible Institute) looks down a side street toward the old Genesee Road.

Lima's historic character is promoted by a vibrant historical society and its walking tour brochure. Preservation sometimes happens when places get snubbed. Lima was bypassed first by the Erie Canal, then by the railroad. Developers and big change went elsewhere. It happened in 1870 to Genesee College, which relocated to Syracuse where it became Syracuse University.

Not far from Lima, near the intersection with Livonia Center Road, Routes 5 and 20 slice alongside Fort Hill, site of a Seneca palisaded village destroyed by a French–Algonquin military expedition in 1697. Traces of stockade earthworks may still be found on the wooded crest of the hill. After white settlers began trickling into the area, around 1796 a tavern called the Yellow Wasp appeared at the foot of the hill. It became an entertainment mecca through the nineteenth century. The Wasp's dance floor was supported on a concoction of twenty-four wagon springs presumably scavenged from casualties of the rutted road. The inn operated until 1906. It leaves only the trace of an overgrown driveway.

The village of Avon sits on high ground above where the Genesee Road met its namesake, a river flowing north from Pennsylvania's Allegheny Mountains to Lake Ontario. Routes 5 and 20, still running together, cross the river roughly where Native Americans forded from time immemorial (both river and ford no doubt shifted over centuries). Algonquins, Haudenosaunee, European explorers, fur traders, surveyors, homesteaders, they all forded the river (or crossed by canoe) until Gilbert and Maria Berry arrived from Geneva in 1789, Avon's first white settlers. They rigged up a rope ferry and built a tavern just south of the current bridge. The first bridge came with the turnpike in 1804. Two years later it was carried away by flood waters, rebuilt, and washed away again in 1816 just after carrying troops home from war with British Canada.

Across the river, Canawaugus was the last significant, traditional Seneca village on the old trail west. The name has been translated as "stinking waters," referring to aromas wafting across the river from sulfur springs on the site of what became Avon. Stinking water turned Avon into what some called "the new Saratoga." It began with the Wadsworth family, the first white settlers of the Genesee. Among a number of farms they established along the river, one contained a spring now located in an Avon village park. In 1821, one of the Wadsworths erected a family "shower box" to bathe in the spring's mineral waters—the unwitting birth of a small-town industry. The box grew into a popular public bathhouse, soon followed by hotels. More than a dozen hotels were scattered between various springs around town by the late 1800s. Some aspired to the *cachet* of Saratoga, some took the curative effects of sulfur treatment more seriously, but virtually all were gone by the end of the century, burned down or burned out as the spa trend waned.

Only the Avon Inn survives, a striking Greek Revival on the old road as it approaches Avon's central circle. Built as a private home around 1840, it became one of the village's famous spa inns toward the end of the glory days, losing only an upper story to fire. Today the Avon Inn's website barely mentions the historic curative springs, which indeed have all either been capped or funneled away, no longer wanted. At least one, however, can still be tracked down from a gazebo in Avon's Driving Park, with a bit of nosing around.

The Genesee River was the end of the road for thousands of settlers in the 1790s and early 1800s. They turned the valley into an early American breadbasket. But as the river corridor filled with farms, homesteaders kept coming. And new territories beckoned—Western New York, Ohio. Sadly, some of the continued migration involved poor farming practices endemic at a time of fertile new horizons—little attention paid to crop rotation or managing fertility. There was so much more land out there. Too often the thinking was: exploit what's here and move on.

6

Across the River

Shortly after crossing the Genesee, Routes 5 and 20 go their separate ways. They have overlapped for the last sixty miles since Auburn. Route 20 originated as the Great Western Turnpike, a rival of the Seneca Turnpike built in stages during the early decades of the 1800s. It, too, largely followed Indian trails but on a much straighter course, south of the Mohawk Valley, freed from the river's twists and turns. After the conjoined roads cross the Genesee, Route 20 takes the western pike's relatively straight line to Buffalo while Route 5 generally follows the old Indian path toward the Niagara. At this point the Seneca Turnpike became the Ontario and Genesee Turnpike, but it was still often called the Genesee Road, or Buffalo Road.

About a mile after NY 20 turns away, Route 5 comes to an historical marker for the Seneca village of Canawaugus, at an intersection with River Road. Canawaugus played a particularly significant role in affairs surrounding the American Revolution. It was home to around a thousand Senecas, among them three prominent figures in the Iroquois Confederacy: Cornplanter, one of the key negotiators of treaties; his half-brother Handsome Lake, a prophet and spiritual leader of Haudenosaunee religious revival; and their nephew Chainbreaker, a warrior-chief who led deadly raids against settlers during the war.

These three men made Canawaugus the site of Iroquois councils with deep implications for the future of the Haudenosaunee and white settlers. Handsome Lake's teachings and moral code are still alive in the Iroquois Longhouse Religion. The cultural significance of Canawaugus recently energized a protest movement against burying the historic site under a massive solar farm.

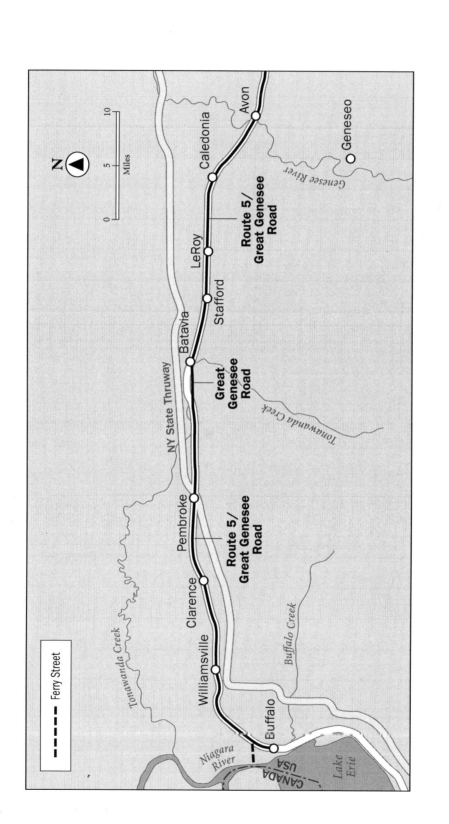

Handsome Lake/Ganiodaiio (1735–1815)

Sometime around 1814 the Seneca prophet Handsome Lake set out on the old Iroquois Trail for a long walk to the council village of the Onondaga. He was almost eighty years old, accompanied by a small group of followers. They camped one night at Canawaugus, the village of his birth on the Genesee River, and another night at Ganundasaga, near Geneva. As word spread about his vision, that he would go to Onondaga to die, many more people joined the march. They must have encountered waves of homesteaders and soldiers headed west on the Genesee Road.

The Onondaga celebrated Handsome Lake's arrival with a game of lacrosse, but he was distracted, depressed, unable to speak about his visions and teachings. He became gravely ill and died in 1815.

There is almost nothing known about his early life. He was a half-brother of the Seneca chief Cornplanter. The name Handsome Lake appears on the Canandaigua Treaty of 1794, in which the United States government pledged never to claim the Seneca land "nor disturb that Seneca nation, nor any of the Six Nations, or their Indian friends residing thereon." It is unclear if Handsome Lake played any role in negotiations. In any case, the abrogation of that treaty and many others, and the relentless displacement of the Haudenosaunee people from their land and culture, drove him into years of despair, alcoholism, abject poverty, and sickness. He later said that he became "as dead" when he was visited by "four beings" who revealed to him the will of the Creator.

Those quoted words come from the foreword of the Code of Handsome Lake, a transcript of teachings and prophecies preserved by his descendants and followers. His message was in essence a plan for survival of the Haudenosaunee people— spiritual, cultural, and physical—within an alien civilization. It was a complex mix of resistance and reconciliation. He preached temperance, peace, refusal to sell land, and an end to some aspects of Haudenosaunee matriarchy. He criticized some traditional religious beliefs but argued against adopting Christianity. And he advised men that they would need to give up their hunting ways and learn from white men how to farm.

Handsome Lake visited Washington, DC, in 1802 with a delegation of Seneca and Onondaga chiefs. President Jefferson later sent a letter to the Haudenosaunee people praising Handsome Lake's message of reform, but the prophet was more controversial within the Iroquois community. Some chiefs vilified him for turning his back on traditional religion. Red Jacket called him an impostor.

Cornplanter was sometimes skeptical about his brother, but in the end he said, "He made mistakes, many mistakes, so it is reported, but he was only a man and men are liable to commit errors. Whatever he did and said of himself is of no consequence. What he did and said by the direction of the four messengers is everything—it is our religion. Ganiodaiio was weak in many points and sometimes afraid to do as the messengers told him. He was almost an unwilling servant. He made no divine claims, he did not pose as infallible nor even truly virtuous. . . . We do not worship him, we worship one great Creator."

Land agent Charles Williamson had his eye on another Seneca encampment a few miles past Canawaugus. "Big Springs" was the name given to a place visited annually for centuries, where very cold springs fed a twenty-acre pond teeming with trout. Not a village per se, this was a traditional campground during fishing season.

Williamson invited Scottish settlers to come to Big Springs in 1799, giving the place the Roman name for their (and his) British homeland: Caledonia. A couple of years later he put a grist mill at the outlet of the pond. Peter Campbell was one of the half-dozen first settlers. In 1805, he built a timber-frame house near the mill. It still stands, with original clapboard siding and twelve-over-eight windows, but not in Caledonia. The house was moved two miles north to Genesee Country Village, a recreated community of rescued nineteenth-century buildings.

The fish pond of campground days had shrunk to two acres on an 1870s map. It's completely gone now, drained and filled-in for a neighborhood of homes. An outcrop of limestone south of the village provided an easy supply of building stone that is evident today in a number of two-century-old stone buildings along Main Street. The Caledonia Public Library occupies one of them: the house of Gad Blakeslee, an officer in the War of 1812, built in 1826. It served as the village's first post office.

At about the same time, James Clark built the most impressive tavern on the turnpike for many miles in either direction. The Clark Tavern is a classic case of what so often happens over the years to second-generation taverns built on the turnpike: they typically replaced the log cabins and simple frame houses that took in early travelers. They became centers of new village life: stagecoach stations, meeting places, post offices, dance halls, courtrooms, banks. When those functions moved on to their own buildings, the old taverns, if they survived, might eventually house a historical society or a private residence, as the Clark house did in the 1930s. Almost a hundred years later, with original features still intact but badly needing restoration, the Clark Tavern went up for sale in 2022 for $59,000—a very old, demanding house on the main street of a rural, upstate village, perhaps a little too far outside the sphere of big-city commuters.

In the 1820s, this was perhaps the finest tavern on the turnpike in Genesee country. It looked out across the road at a small lake known as Big Springs. Most of the second floor was a double-arched ballroom. Over the years it served as a stagecoach stop, post office, bank, and Caledonia's library before becoming an elegant private home in the 1930s. Seen here empty in 2022, the building still retained original features but was badly deteriorated, desperate for a buyer. *Photo by the author.*

One block away, looking down Main Street, the three-story Masonic Temple opened in 1831 as the Caledonia House, a business venture of stone mason James Shaw, known in its day as "the Stone Hotel." After only a few short years, a "hotel" was upstaging a "tavern."

When Caledonia's spring pond was still around, in the early 1860s, a celebrated angler and commercial fish merchant from Rochester, Seth Green, bought property along the pond's outlet brook. Using the pure, cold water once fished by the Seneca, Green established the first fish-farming operation in the western hemisphere. "We have tilled the ground 4,000 years," he wrote, "we have just begun to till the water." The successful facility was taken over by the state in 1875 and continues today as New York's largest fish hatchery, supplying brown and rainbow trout to stock lakes and ponds throughout the state. The hatchery's compound of Victorian-era structures has been designated a historic district, and Seth Green is considered "the father of fish culture in North America."

Several miles before LeRoy, the next village after Caledonia, Route 5 passes by the first pioneer cemetery west of the Genesee, an unmarked plot with a couple of dozen headstones known to locals as the Buell Burying Ground. At its center, an elegantly carved stone marks the grave of Brigadier General Daniel Davis, "killed back of Fort Erie at the Sortie from the Fort" in 1814. The stone is slate; it must have been brought here from many miles east, and although slate is more durable than the local lime-stone, it is beginning to delaminate and crumble along with Daniel Davis's bones.

Like many other New Englanders, after the Revolution Davis left his colonial family farm when generations of heirs had divided it into unsustainable fragments. He was

A boy growing up near Rochester in the early 1800s learned the art and skills of fishing from his Seneca neighbors. For centuries Senecas had gathered annually at a nearby spring-fed fishing pond. Seth Green bought that property years later and established the first fish hatchery in the western hemisphere. He is regarded as the father of fish culture in North America. The state bought the hatchery in 1875 and built this fish barn surrounded in ponds, today nurturing 170,000 pounds of brown and rainbow trout a year to stock waters around the state. *New York State Department of Environmental Conservation.*

twenty-two years old in 1799, lured by "Genesee Fever," purchasing land a few miles past the new settlement of Caledonia. Two years later he joined a local militia. When the second war with Britain came, he was called to action as the militia's commanding officer. Months later he was killed in one of the last battles of the war.

A few miles beyond the cemetery, at one edge of the LeRoy Country Club, a sign marks the site of an outpost that enticed Daniel Davis. A log tavern appeared here in 1793, run by a squatter named Charles Wilbur. He was probably the first white settler west of the Genesee River. There weren't even many Iroquois living in this area; there was nowhere else for a traveler on the trail to find shelter, but there were so few travelers that Wilbur sold his tavern a few years later to a veteran of the Sullivan campaign: Captain John Ganson. He had experience operating a sawmill. He replaced the logs with a wood-framed tavern, attracting a trickle of homesteaders like Daniel Davis to build framed cabins along the road. Ganson's Settlement was the first white community west of the Genesee.

What remains of Ganson Tavern is just a dirt lane to an empty lot overlooking a golf course. The legacy of Ganson's Settlement is the village of LeRoy, built-up around a place where the Genesee Road crossed nearby Oatka Creek. Oatka is the largest tributary of the Genesee. Route 5, LeRoy's Main Street, follows the original crossing almost directly over a drop in the creek called Old Buttermilk Falls. At the end of the bridge, the village post office occupies the site of a mill opened in 1803. Across the street is a stone tavern built during the turnpike years, probably the 1820s. After soldiering through the centuries recycled as a hat factory, a bank, private residence, and doctor's office, and suffering a near-fatal fire in 2004, it underwent a million-dollar rebirth in 2019 as the Farmer's Creekside Tavern & Inn.

The village name LeRoy comes from Herman LeRoy, one of the most prominent late-eighteenth-century merchants and financiers in New York City. He and associates purchased eighty-five-thousand acres of Western New York from Robert Morris in 1793, when Morris still didn't have clear title from the Seneca Nation. This was the same year squatter Charles Wilbur built his tavern. LeRoy didn't take legal ownership for a few more years (legality may still be in dispute). He never did visit the property, but his son Jacob took an interest, building a land office on the Genesee Road near the bridge.

That 1822 office, soon expanded into a grand house for Jacob LeRoy, is now a museum of the LeRoy Historical Society. In the 1850s, after the land office closed, it was home to the chancellor of the village's Ingham University, the first women's university in the nation (closed in 1892). Behind the house, another museum building highlights the various enterprises—makers of plows, patent medicines, salt, limestone, educated women, railroad cars—that grew LeRoy from a farming community into the handsome village it is today. The stringless bean was one of LeRoy's gifts to the world.

After ten years meeting in homes, barns, and schoolhouses, people of LeRoy spent three years building a simple, meeting-house-style church with bell tower in 1825, on the Genesee Road uphill from Oatka Creek. It soon became a touchstone for antislavery sentiment heating up in Western New York. In the course of two centuries the church has grown Italianate with Classical Revival embellishments, but it still retains a simple elegance. *Photo by the author.*

But the village takes special pride as the home of Jell-O, devoting most of the museum to the story of how "America's most famous dessert" made a fortune for LeRoy entrepreneur Orator Woodward. When the Woodward family chose a site for their mansion at the edge of town, they tore down the old Ganson Tavern.

THE TREATY OF BIG TREE

In the early 1790s, Philadelphia financier and land speculator Robert Morris claimed ownership of nearly four million acres of New York State, based on his purchase of land rights from the state of Massachusetts. He had been the richest man in America, but by this time he found himself overextended, land poor, and facing bankruptcy. He needed to liquidate assets. In 1793, he sold the western end of New York to a syndicate of Dutch bankers and investors, the Holland Land Company. It was a miraculous deal because Morris didn't actually own any of this land. It was legal property of the Seneca Nation. Massachusetts had only sold him the exclusive right to buy land from the Senecas.

Morris now had many times more than enough money to buy the land he had already sold. This was the convoluted backdrop to the Treaty of Big Tree, negotiated in September 1797 at one of the enormous oak trees along the Genesee River. At the time, the western end of the Great Genesee Road, beyond the river, was still little more than a native path through wilderness linking some Iroquois camps or settlements, a few scattered huts of white squatters and traders, and four or five crude houses on the shore of Lake Erie.

Morris made elaborate preparations for the treaty council fire, arranging for ox carts loaded with food, presents, and barrels of whiskey, dispatched from Albany on the Genesee Road and from Philadelphia along the new road cut by Charles Williamson. A small herd of cattle and hogs accompanied the carts. The processions served as general invitations to a great feast. Some three thousand Seneca and members of other Iroquois Nations came, led by prominent Seneca sachems, principal warriors, and clan matriarchs. They converged on the site near today's Geneseo days ahead of the official white delegation. Morris sent his son Thomas and his friend Charles Williamson as chief negotiators. The federal government was represented by Jeremiah Wadsworth, patriarch of the first white settlement on the Genesee. Horatio Jones served as a translator. Various uninvited whites also showed up to see what they could do.

Morris instructed his son to offer the Seneca $75,000 for almost four million acres between the river, Lake Erie, Pennsylvania, and Lake Ontario, allowing for some "not very large" reservations around native villages. He noted, "The Indians must have plenty of food, and also of liquor, when you see it proper to order it for them." The provisions included 1,500 rations of whiskey—"if not sufficient more must be got." He also authorized a sliding scale of gifts: "500 or 600 dollars or if necessary 1,000 dollars, for the chiefs," payable after the treaty was signed.

Cornplanter, Farmer's Brother, and especially Red Jacket initially spoke against the sale of land and creation of reservations. Thomas Morris countered with lavish terms but held back on specifics. Negotiations dragged on for more than two weeks. Fights broke out when whiskey made its way into the Iroquois camp. A white instigator was taken off to jail in Canandaigua. Red Jacket proposed selling six square miles along the Pennsylvania border, immediately rejected by Morris. The chiefs walked away from the council fire. Morris then took a group of Seneca matriarchs aside, distributed presents, and pressed for a reconciliation. They revived the council.

In the end, talks led by Cornplanter settled on a payment of $100,000 (not including bribes) for 3,750,000 acres, excluding about 200,000 acres for eleven scattered reservations. One of these would encompass the village of Canawaugus on the river, bounded on one side by the Genesee Road. Fifty-two Senecas signed the treaty document (with Xs). Cornplanter received the largest secret "annuity": $250 annually for life. Robert Morris now had his deed for the Holland Land Company.

A centennial celebration of the treaty was held at Geneseo in 1897. During the accolades for civilization's march across the great state of New York, one speaker raised the tender subject of bribery: "if Red Jacket, Cornplanter, Little Billy, Pollard, Farmer's Brother and Young King received gratuities, pensions or bribes, ranging from $10 to $250 per annum for their influences with their people to effect a sale, are they any more to be blamed than Thomas Morris, acting under the deliberate and explicit directions of his illustrious father? In a case of bribery, it is not always easy to determine which is the guiltier, the briber or the bribee."

By 1897, the eleven reservations had been stripped of almost three-quarters of their land. Another hundred years later, the village of Canawaugus, home of Cornplanter and Handsome Lake, was abandoned and its reservation, along with several others, no longer appeared on maps. One of the largest reservations, at Buffalo Creek, was officially completely dissolved and swallowed up by the city of Buffalo. In 2010, Senecas bought nine acres of land once part of that reservation from a real estate developer (calling himself the Ellicott Development Company) to build the Seneca Buffalo Creek Casino and a convenience store.

7

The Holland Land Company

The hamlet of Stafford, four miles from LeRoy, is a farming crossroads that accumulated a population of more than 2,500 by 1840 and has never had that many residents since. Stafford's four-corners intersection has a "captured-in-amber" feeling about it. Three of the corners have nineteenth-century buildings with towers—a church, an erstwhile town hall, and a tattered, abandoned general store. On the fourth corner a tiny park commemorates an astonishing number of Stafford men who served and died in half a dozen wars. It gives the impression most of the village's future was killed off in war after war.

One section of a private home next to the town hall is said to be the oldest house in Genesee County. What looks like a blacksmith shop squats next to the bridge over a small creek.

The crossroad at Stafford's four-corners is called Transit Road (Route 237), a road with a history rivaling this section of the Great Genesee. When a survey was begun here in 1798—using a transit—the straight, north–south line followed by this road was set as an eastern boundary of the last major New York land purchase from the Haudenosaunee, encompassing the entire western end of the state. The line ran from Lake Ontario to Pennsylvania. The first survey crew came out the Iroquois Trail from Lake Erie: two surveyors carrying a transit on horseback accompanied by a dozen men with axes. They established where the trail crossed the eastern edge of the land purchase, set up camp, and began cutting a straight swath through the forest, north and south from the trail, wide enough for their primitive instrument to take sight-line readings over the terrain.

Imagine traveling a wilderness path from the east and suddenly coming upon a thirty-foot gap in the trees as far as the eye could see in either direction, something like the firebreaks cleared through woodlands today. A storehouse established at this point on the trail during the three-year-long survey grew into the first white settlement this far west. It was sensibly named Transit. Years later there came an influx of British homesteaders, and though they were in the *transition* of their lives, they decided to change the name Transit to Stafford, after the village they had left in Shropshire.

On the outskirts of Stafford, in the front lawn of a Town Highway Garage, the road passes by a very odd rock: a pillar of limestone about nine feet high in the arresting shape of a toadstool. Known for untold years as "Devil's Rock," it intrigued passersby long enough to promulgate its own myth. It seems Beelzebub, weary from a long walk on the trail, took a nap against the rock. Someone (by some accounts a band of angels) came along, saw an opportunity, carefully tied a chain around the devil's waist, and looped the other end around the rock. When he woke up, furious, he ran around and around the rock until the chain wore down its middle to form a limestone mushroom.

Perhaps Satan was so upset he sent the men of Stafford off to battlefields. Or maybe he put a curse on the next village up the road: Batavia—plagued through the years by flooding from Tonawanda Creek and now immersed in miles of commercial sprawl.

Between Stafford and Batavia, Route 5—continuing the path of the Iroquois Trail and Genesee Road—passes into the watershed of the Niagara River. Tonawanda Creek is the primary tributary of the Niagara, meeting it above the famous falls. The creek, ten times longer than the river, draws a broad arc through Western New York. About midway through that arc it makes a sharp bend. This spot was a traditional Seneca meeting place, where the Iroquois Trail split, one path crossing the creek west to Lake Erie, the other angling north toward the Niagara River and Lake Ontario.

The Holland Land Company put a sales office at this bend of Tonawanda Creek in 1801. A group of Dutch bankers and investors had formed the company to purchase three-and-a-quarter million acres of Western New York from the millionaire American speculator Robert Morris (who had previously sold land to Herman LeRoy, and before that, land east of the Genesee to the Pulteney British syndicate).

The Dutch company named their outpost "Batavia" in honor of a period of republican government in the Netherlands. They hired a surveyor named Joseph Ellicott to fix the eastern boundary of the enormous tract (at Transit) and carve it into sellable

The limestone escarpment that underlies much of Route 5 pokes up just west of Stafford in this arresting form. A rock that strange likely served as a marker along the Native American path and certainly did on the old road. It cried out for a backstory, supplied early on in the local myth of "Devil's Rock." It seems Beelzebub grew weary along the path, took a nap at the rock, was quietly chained to it by passersby, woke up enraged, and ran tethered in circles until a pillar wore down to a limestone toadstool. *Photo by the author.*

lots. Ellicott had recently worked with two brothers, also surveyors, marking boundaries of the District of Columbia for the new federal city of Washington. He finished three years crisscrossing the Holland Land Purchase in 1801, and that year the company opened for business in a log-cabin sales office on the creek, more or less at the site of the Iroquois campground. Also that year Ellicott had a sawmill built nearby, and a gristmill a few years later as lots began selling. He began building a series of roads radiating in all directions from Batavia, for settlers carrying deeds to plots of land scattered through Western New York. Maps today show Batavia at the center of this starburst of roads.

Runners

When the Holland Land Office was just beginning to sell plots at Batavia, one of the settlers needed to sign a document he had left back in Avon. This was before any stagecoach service or mail delivery west of the Genesee, so he engaged a young Seneca man from the nearby Tonawanda Reservation literally to run an errand and fetch the document. The Seneca courier left Tonawanda at daybreak, ran to Avon, and brought the document back in Batavia by midday, a distance of more than sixty miles: a good morning run.

Foot racing, especially relay races, are a traditional part of Haudenosaunee entertainment and culture. The runner summoned councils, conveyed intelligence between nations, carried warnings of danger. For energy he wore a deerskin pouch with pounded corn and maple sugar.

But the Batavia operation shut down when war broke out with Britain in 1812, at the Holland Land Company's very doorstep. British troops burned an American fort and settlement at Buffalo Creek on Lake Erie. Residents there fled inland on the road to Batavia. The land office and nearby houses were inundated with refugees uncertain if the British would soon be following. Life around Batavia became tenuous until the war ended.

When peace did come, the land company replaced the old office with the substantial fieldstone building on the site today in a small memorial park. Backed against Tonawanda Creek, the building later grew wings and a Greek Revival portico, but the original simple, stone structure is well preserved. And it is packed with exhibits, artifacts, and backstories. The Batavia Historical Society was formed in the 1890s specifically to save this seminal piece of village history from demolition.

The earliest maps of the Holland Purchase show the road to Buffalo splitting when it reached Tonawanda Creek, proceeding along both banks. The main Iroquois Trail probably crossed the creek at the campground, leading to what is now Batavia's South Main Street on that side of the creek. An alternate path ran along the north bank, as Route 5 does today for about a mile until it is joined by South Main. The way these two routes ran parallel on either side of the creek recalls the two paths along the Seneca River between Cayuga and Seneca Lakes. In both cases early travelers had two options for fording the water depending on conditions at the time of year—low or high water, ice-over, and so on. Like the Seneca River example, the north-bank road in Batavia (Route 5) has become a commercial corridor while the road south of the creek takes a quieter turn from residential to rural.

When the Holland Land Company built this limestone office in 1815, Batavia was the hub for land sales and settlement throughout Western New York. People streamed in and out of this door staking their claims and venturing off to start new lives. Twenty years later a mob of angry farmers stormed the office, furious that Dutch investors and their local cronies were bleeding mortgaged residents. The company folded in 1839. The building then went into a too-familiar series of repurposes, decline, and abandonment, until a drive to save it sparked the creation of the Batavia Historical Society. *Holland Land Office Museum.*

Headed west from Batavia, the old path followed Tonawanda Creek, as Route 5 does, for several miles. Near the hamlet of Bushville, Willow Bend Inn claims to be a stagecoach tavern "established in 1790." There were no taverns or houses along here at that time, and not even much of a road. The first stagecoach wouldn't come along for another fifteen years.

At East Pembroke, Route 5 leaves the creek to continue due west toward Lake Erie. In a short distance the road passes alongside a stone wall enclosing a small field. An alley of old trees leads uphill to a farm. Nearby a sign marks the site of one of the early purchases of land from the Holland Company by David Goss, an immigrant from Massachusetts in 1804. Goss's gravestone may be one of the weathered slabs in the hilltop Old Buffalo Road Cemetery just up the road.

Foundation remnants of a mill sit alongside Route 5 as it crosses Murder Creek in the hamlet of Pembroke. The grim name comes from a gothic tale of an Indian maiden and her lover pursued along the creek by an embittered rival.

The road glides across gentle undulations of farmland until it drops abruptly into the village of Clarence, formerly known as Clarence Hollow, and before that, Ransomville. A Massachusetts silversmith named Asa Ransom came here in 1799 after spending several years among the squatters at Seneca Lake, reportedly "engaged in manufacturing Indian trinkets" for traders. He needed a legitimate home. His chance came when Joseph Ellicott, agent of the Holland Land Company, was authorized "to contract with six reputable persons to locate themselves on the road from the Eastern Transit [Stafford] to Buffalo Creek, about ten miles distant from one another, and open houses of entertainment for travelers, promising to such persons a deed of from fifty to one hundred and fifty acres of land each, at a liberal time of payment without interest, at the lowest price the company will sell lands when settlement shall be begun." Among the first men responding to Ellicott's offer, Frederick Walthurs opened a tavern at the storehouse clearing on the transit line and Asa Ransom chose the hollow.

As Clarence's Main Street (Route 5) bottoms out, it comes to a time-worn but still-imposing stone building bearing the date 1810. Now a private residence, this was once an early, genteel hotel, but it wasn't Ransom's hotel. His "house of entertainment for travelers" was located a few blocks further on.

A shingle in front of "Asa Random Inn" marks the spot; but again, this isn't Asa's original inn. This handsome B&B was built in 1853 on the four-foot-thick foundation walls of the original. A year prior, the older inn was jacked up and moved a quarter-mile east, to a lot above where the road begins its descent into the hollow. There the original sits today: a large, white, New England–style saltbox, now a private home. The reason for the move is unclear. It must have been quite a spectacle to watch horses or oxen pull this big house through the village and up the hill.

Behind the Asa Ransom Inn are ruins of a gristmill Asa built in 1803, with the skeleton of a railroad trestle connected to the mill in the late 1800s. A dam and mill pond are part of a village park just up the road. The park also contains the Clarence Historical Museum and, next to it, a rare, surviving example of the log cabins of the region's first white settlers, in this case a Massachusetts farmer named Levi Goodrich. He built his round-log, saddle-notched hut in the 1820s while he worked a side-line surveying local roads, including his own Goodrich Road. The homestead cabin even-

Massachusetts silversmith Asa Ransom arrived at Clarence Hollow in 1799, lured by a
generous deal from the Holland Land Company. He was the first white settler this far
west on the road. Four years later, behind
his tavern he built a gristmill. One corner of
the mill's ruins are moldering behind today's
charming Asa Ransom Inn, an 1853 replace-
ment on the site of the original. In the late
1800s, the railroad ran a spur to the mill's
tower, leaving the skeleton of a trestle visible
on the left. *Photo by the author.*

At Clarence's village park on Route 5 (in the
background), a rare, two-century-old log cabin
was moved here in 1990 from a few miles
away. It had been part of a large house on a
prosperous farm evolved from the homestead
of a Massachusetts emigrant. The round-
log, saddle-notched walls are typical of first-
settler cabins, though here the interior walls
were hewn flat for a little refinement and
whitewashed with lime. The cabin is open to
visitors as part of the Clarence Historical Museum. *Photo by the author.*

tually became part of a large, frame house as the farm grew and prospered. The Clarence Historical Society purchased the cabin in 1990, broke it off, restored, and moved
it to the village park.

Travelers on the road through Ransomville around the turn of the nineteenth
century were often headed to Canada. Many were Haudenosaunee families carrying
their bundled, broken lives. They did not stop at Ransom's inn. Some travelers who
did stop were diehard, Canada-bound British Loyalists losing hope that the American
experiment would collapse.

Not all Tories chose to leave the country; many still believed, at least until 1815, that
Britain would prevail in the end. British sympathy and allegiance lingered especially in
Western New York, reflected in names adopted by local villages. Clarence was named
after a son of King George III (later taking the throne as William IV). Amherst was
named for Lord Jeffrey Amherst, victorious general of the French and Indian War.

Clarence is the last distinct, semirural village before Route 5 enters the developed environs of Buffalo City. In the shadow of Buffalo Niagara International Airport, suburban Williamsville has struggled to hold on to its heritage. The village's Historic Preservation Commission lists more than two dozen landmark properties along Main Street. The oldest is the Williamsville Water Mill, just off Main on Ellicott Creek. It was built in 1811 by the village's namesake settler Jonas Williams. In the 1820s, it was converted from gristmill to a cement business for construction of the Erie Canal, but it returned to grinding flour until 1947. The village rescued it from decay in 2005.

When the British army burned the village of Buffalo in 1813, a young carpenter, Oziek Smith, fled with his family to Williamsville. He bought Jonas Williams's log cabin on the Old Buffalo Road, became one of the area's prominent entrepreneurs, and established what is now its oldest continuously operated tavern, the Eagle House. He constructed the tavern between 1827 and 1832, installing an upstairs, curved-ceiling, spring-floored ballroom. It burned down when still unfinished while he was away on business, and he immediately rebuilt on the same foundation. On a farm outside the village Smith grew his own hops. The walls of today's restaurant are lined with old photos and memorabilia. There is evidence that chambers and passages in the cellar, extending under the road, were used in the Underground Railroad.

The Eagle House is close to Ellicott Creek. In the early years, spring floods kept washing out the creek's plank bridges. They were finally replaced in 1882 by a double-arched, stone bridge built to last. Remarkably, it carries Route 5 traffic through busy Williamsville to this day.

After Williamsville, Route 5 gradually curves from west to south as Main Street enters the city of Buffalo. About midway through that arc, West Ferry Street turns off toward the Niagara River. There were two ferry crossings to Canada near the river's Lake Erie outlet. The Black Rock Ferry—named for a huge outcrop of black chert and limestone along the riverbank—started operating ad hoc during the Revolution, at the end of the lake (the Peace Bridge crosses there today). Construction of the Erie Canal destroyed the ferry landing (and the black rock outcrop) in 1824.

The ferry then relocated half a mile downriver. There it continued running for 120 years, leaving from the end of Ferry Street. The old ferry had been a rowing scow. The new boat was mandated by the state to be horse-powered. The ferryman went to Albany for machinery: a horizontal treadwheel big enough for four horses, with cogs engaging a propellor shaft. It was only the second such contraption in the country. A dozen years later the horses were replaced by a steam engine.

A small, quiet park commemorates the ferry landing at the tip of Unity Island. It looks out at the Peace Bridge, the Canadian shoreline, and a daunting mass of water spilling from four Great Lakes. This was the crossing made by untold numbers of fugitive slaves in the decades before the Civil War. A small interpretive center at the park tells the story, and a meditation garden invites people to ponder.

The island park is separated from the shore by a channel of the Erie Canal, spanned by a heel-trunnion bascule bridge. Its single steel deck is hinged at one end to swing up like a trap door. It was built in 1913–1914 from plans by an engineer-inventor named Joseph Baermann Strauss, who went on to oversee construction of the Golden Gate and George Washington Bridges.

After Main Street passes Ferry Street, in about ten blocks it comes to North Street. Originally called Guide Board Road, it followed a native path to the river canoe-crossing at the end of the lake. In the 1790s, the path was opened for wagons to the first ferry, while the rest of Main Street remained a trail for several more years. A description of that trail comes from William Peacock, recollecting (in the early 1800s) a trip he took to Buffalo Creek as a nineteen-year-old:

> In passing down along the Indian path, the land was covered with a very thick underbrush, small timber, and some large old oak trees . . . [they] so overshadowed the path that, when our saddlebags touched a bush, we would be completely drenched with rain after a shower. There was a little cleared spot on the Terrace bank . . . covered with a green sward, on which the Indians, on a fine day, would lie and look off upon Lake Erie. . . . Coming out of the woods, it burst on my vision the large and beautiful sheet of pure water.
>
> [On the Terrace] was erected a log cabin, or house, covered with bark, and occupied by Johnson, a descendant of Sir William Johnson.

The Terrace was a bench of high ground overlooking Buffalo Creek bottomland, roughly on the line of Lower Terrace and Swan Street today. The "descendant" Peacock refers to was Sir Williams's namesake son, William, also known as Tagawirunta, one of the children the baronet sired with his Mohawk consort, Molly Brant. Apparently a favorite, Tagawirunta inherited 100 pounds sterling in Sir Williams's will. He fled the Mohawk Valley to live with Senecas at Buffalo Creek during the Revolution, and he became, by one account, "the leading man at Buffalo Creek at the time of the survey and settlement."

A small team of Holland Land Company surveyors arrived at Buffalo Creek about the same time William Peacock rode in on his horse. The company was initially formed in 1789 by four Dutch bankers, some of whom had made risky loans to the Continental Congress during the Revolution. After their purchase of most of the western end of the state from Robert Morris in 1793, several years were spent sorting things out with the Haudenosaunee, particularly the Seneca. The Seneca village on Buffalo Creek, near its outlet to Lake Erie, had swollen with arrivals of displaced Iroquois.

The creek may have been called "Buffalo" after animals frequented a famous salt lick near the village. Some historians dispute this, pointing out there is no reliable record of buffalo inhabiting the area. But there *are* historical accounts of the animals in Ohio territory, and some believe they may even have once roamed as far east as the Hudson River (no one has put them in New England; that somehow seems unthinkable). In any case, for their new city the Dutch investors dropped the "Buffalo" name in favor of another that had become available since 1674: New Amsterdam.

The first survey of the *new* New Amsterdam site, probably in 1800, shows—in the Dutch way—a grid of canals planned for the bottomland below the Terrace. On higher ground, roads were arranged around a circle and given the names of Hollander investors. Little of this came about. The benchland Terrace, standing nearly forty feet above lake level, was graded down to the creek so that today there is hardly any sense of a slope. People kept calling the place Buffalo Creek until the company gave up on "New Amsterdam" in 1805. "Creek" also dropped away, leaving "Buffalo." And the streets lost their Dutch names when the opening of the Erie Canal transformed the provincial little town into a burgeoning American city. Schimmelpennick became Niagara Street, Vollenhoven Avenue became Erie Street, and Willink and Vanstaphorst Streets became Main Street.

After Buffalo's Metro Rail stops at Church Street, the tram crosses several blocks of what were bottomlands of Buffalo Creek to reach "Canalside," at the end of Main Street. This was a place of minor economic significance until it was declared the western terminus of the Erie Canal. That momentous decision came in 1823 after a bitter,

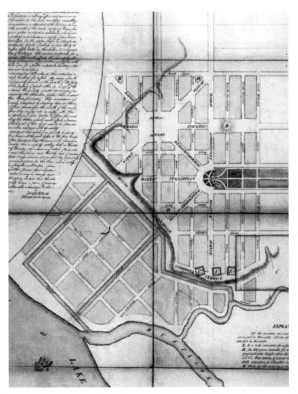

The Holland Land Company had big plans for a city on Lake Erie at the end of the Genesee Road. Once again, North America would have a "New Amsterdam." The company's chief surveyor, Joseph Ellicott, drew up this plan in 1800. It incorporated radial elements of the street layout on which his brother was working at about the same time for the new federal city of Washington. There is also a nod to the network of canals in old Amsterdam. Neither the plan nor the city name took hold, but a similar grid of canals did appear during the heyday of the Erie Canal. *SUNY at Fredonia, Daniel A. Reed Library.*

eleventh-hour fight between proponents of Buffalo Creek and backers of the ferry landing at Black Rock.

Not far from where Main Street meets the creek, the Seneca Buffalo Creek Casino occupies the approximate site of the eighteenth-century Seneca village. That village influenced the final destination of the Great Genesee Road, which in turn influenced the terminus of the Erie Canal.

The story of this part of Buffalo is a classic tale of the tribulations of urban waterfronts. In this case, the Erie Canal ended in a warren of lakeside slips and channels located ironically in exactly the place mapped out in 1800 for canals of New Amsterdam. The area filled up with warehouses, piers, and shipping offices where "canalers," sailors, and teamsters collected their pay at the end of long hauls. This inevitably created a zone of bars, brothels, and raucous dance halls, turning into a notorious den of violence and vice. When railroads syphoned off business from the Erie Canal, seedy tenements were thrown up for the out-of-work Italian immigrants who built and worked the canal. Defunct slips and channels became open sewers, eventually drained, and filled in for alleys or empty lots. Fitful attempts at twentieth-century urban renewal still left a blighted neighborhood until 2005, when visions of a reclaimed heritage waterfront took hold.

The old wharf for sailing sloops and steamships, at the foot of Main Street, has reappeared as a boardwalk. At one end, an excavated Commercial Slip leads to channels of the canal that have been dug back up—short sections rewatered as playgrounds for paddle-boaters and ice-skaters. Foundation ruins of a steamboat-era hotel sit evocatively next to the slip.

Nearby, a $4 million grant from the state helped build a "longshed" to construct a replica of the packet boat that took Governor DeWitt Clinton from Buffalo to New

Where Erie Lake steamships once docked on Buffalo Creek, the city created a canalside boardwalk in 2008. The pedestrian Central Wharf celebrates "the terminus of the Erie Canal." It could also celebrate the end of the road that linked Lake Erie with the Hudson River long before the canal. That road—Buffalo's Main Street—terminates at the south end of the boardwalk, near a gigantic, stone-walled sandbox and a century-old carousel powered by the sun. *Creative Commons ShareAlike 4.0 International.*

York City on the canal's maiden run. People could look down at the reconstruction in progress from a balcony.

The other end of the Canalside boardwalk, where Main Street meets Buffalo Creek, features a pavilion enclosing a marvelous, century-old carousel. It was moved here from a barn in Tonawanda where it sat in storage for fifty years.

A ride on wooden horses might be a good way to celebrate the long road trip from Albany, even if there is no sign anywhere that this is the end of the Great Genesee Road—the first road across the state of New York.

A big, fragile man. *Holland Land Office Museum.*

Joseph Ellicott (1760–1826)

Joseph Ellicott honed his surveying skills working with his older brother Andrew, chief surveyor for the new federal district being laid out on the Potomac River. The two brothers took over work on the radial design of streets for Washington when the city's master planner Pierre L'Enfant ran afoul of commissioners. Joseph went on to survey a troubled boundary between the state of Georgia and the Creek Nation. Experience on the frontier recommended him to the Holland Land Company, negotiating the purchase of more than three million acres of Seneca land in Western Pennsylvania and New York.

The company hired Ellicott in 1797 to survey boundary lines from the Genesee River to Lake Erie. He in turn hired eleven more surveyors and a team of more than one hundred draftsmen, axmen, cooks, and miscellaneous camp workers. He was a meticulous administrator, provisioner, and bean counter; a hard worker himself and a hard-driving boss. A coworker described him as "short-tempered, somewhat tactless . . . rather dictatorial." He kept the men grumbling as snow piled up in bitter cold. At negotiations for the Treaty of Big Tree, settling issues of land ownership with the Seneca Nation, Ellicott looked after the interests of his company.

When what was called "the Great Survey" wrapped up in October 1800, the company appointed him Resident-Agent, charged with selling off their land for quick profits. They preferred that he find speculative buyers of big tracts, but he ended up selling mostly smaller lots to homesteaders, attempting to lure them by scattering the Genesee Road with inns and mills. He projected selling 150,000 acres within two years. Barely 15,000 sold. Populating the wilderness proved to be a tough slog. Ellicott was an early booster of plans for the Erie Canal, with its enormous promise for developing the Holland Purchase. He served as a Canal Commissioner and facilitated a contribution of more than 100,000 acres of company land to the state for canal construction.

In his zeal to see the land settled and productive, Ellicott was generous with buyers, requiring small down payments, offering lenient terms on mortgages, sometimes extending or forgiving interest payments when families struggled. Land sales fluctuated year to year through the first two decades, and company revenues stalled. The Hollanders weren't happy. Eventually they imposed harsher demands on settlers, raising fees, calling in mortgages. Irate farmers threatened to storm land offices. Poor Ellicott took blame from all sides. He was dismissed in 1821.

A big man—six foot three, burly, driven—Joseph Ellicott was also a fragile man, prone to spells of "melancholy." He never married. After leaving the Holland Land Company his depression grew steadily worse until family members committed him to a mental hospital in New York City, the Bloomingdale Insane Asylum. He traveled there on the just-completed canal he had helped promote and fund. At the asylum, a year later, he hanged himself in a closet.

THE ROAD, THE CANAL, AND THE RAILROAD

For nearly half its 363 miles, the original Erie Canal shadowed the Great Genesee Road. Starting from Schenectady, the dual route followed the Mohawk River to Utica. From there, while the road broke off to the west, the canal stayed with the river to Rome, then looped down to Canastota and paralleled the road again until reaching Chittenango. There the canal and the old road parted ways, the former headed to the new cities of Syracuse and Rochester while the road continued to follow the old Native American path. But there was one other congruence. The Seneca–Cayuga Canal—part of the Erie System—partnered a leg of the Genesee Road between Seneca Falls and Geneva.

For 175 years before any of this canal business, the Great Genesee Road had formed the pattern of commerce and infrastructure in central and Western New York—a chain of inns, smithies, sawmills, gristmills. The road's innkeepers, blacksmiths, and especially teamsters vehemently opposed building the Erie Canal. Their voices were no match against the political juggernaut of Governor DeWitt Clinton and allies like the Holland Land Company.

In 1817, many of the same surveyors who had worked on the road twenty years earlier were now back out with their levels and transits, measuring slopes and heights of adjacent land to lay out sections of the proposed canal. When digging and building began, the turnpike along the Mohawk Valley became a service road for hauling equipment, timbers, and stone. The road surface took a beating. Sleds carried supplies in winter, but lack of snow sometimes brought canal construction to a halt.

At the end of eight years, Governor Clinton took his famous ride on the packet boat *Seneca Chief*, carrying a bucket of Lake Erie water to the Atlantic. Along the way he was cheered but also sometimes heckled by folks invested in traffic on the road. They were right to be upset. Virtually overnight, the shipping rate per hundredweight by canal was one-tenth what teamsters charged on the turnpike. And the time it took to move goods from New York City to Buffalo was cut in half, from one month to two weeks. Commerce on the road quickly dropped off. For passengers, however, traveling the road was still faster—by stagecoach, horseback, or carriage. Mail continued moving by stage. In winter, sleds and runners on coaches kept the roads busy while the canal shut down for about five months, frozen over, sometimes drained for maintenance.

Then everything changed—for road and canal—with the advent of railroads. The Mohawk and Hudson Railroad started operating in 1831, only six years after the canal, the first rail line in the state. Its tracks ran parallel to the Kings Road between Albany and Schenectady. The Utica and Schenectady Railroad was chartered by the state in 1833. Its route ran so close to the Mohawk Turnpike that a clause in the charter required the railroad to purchase the road company and keep the turnpike in good repair. But the collection of turnpike tolls kept dropping, profits turned to deficits, and tollgates were eventually abandoned. The road reverted to the state.

Everything changed again when automobiles came along. In their turn, the railroad and the canal bowed to progress. For most of its length, the Great Genesee Road was reborn as New York State Route 5. Commerce came back to the old roadway. With poignant irony, a few shuttered turnpike toll stations even reopened behind roadside, glass-globed gasoline pumps.

Epilogue
Road of Memory

Life on the Genesee Road has ebbed and flowed. We can only speculate about ancient times when it may well have been a principal east–west trail for Algonquin people prior to the incursion of Haudenosaunee culture (sometime before 1500). As the Iroquois Trail, it connected the People of the Longhouse for centuries, binding together the most powerful Indigenous society in eastern North America.

After the American Revolution, the trail became the new nation's first highway for settlement beyond the Appalachian Mountains, and one of the early roads to be turnpiked. But the parallel Erie Canal and then the railroad robbed the Genesee Road of commercial and through-traffic in the 1830s and '40s. As tolls and profits dropped off, turnpikes gave up their charters and the road was taken over by the state. It quieted to a local roadway in the shadow of railroad and canal, until the automobile came along. As cars, in their turn, gradually robbed traffic from the rails, the Old Genesee Road revived, rebranded in most places as Route 5. Tollgates were replaced by gas stations, and turnpike inns by motels.

As it heads west from Utica, Route 5 passes through one county after another named for the Iroquois nation that historically occupied that land—Oneida, Onondaga, Cayuga, Seneca—a guilt-edged homage to the Haudenosaunee? Surrounding counties have the names of New York politicians and generals.

In 1921, civic leaders in communities along the middle section of the Old Genesee Road/Seneca Turnpike got together and proclaimed it the "Road of Memory." They organized a drive to line its shoulders with hundreds of thousands of native trees, reprising an old custom shading travelers on hot summer days. The project began by planting twenty thousand American elm trees between Utica and Syracuse. In 1929 and again in 1930, the state legislature passed a bill authorizing construction of a highway bridge across Cayuga Lake for the Road of Memory reincarnating the historic Cayuga Long Bridge. The legislation caused a flare-up of controversy. Local opposition prompted Governor Franklin Roosevelt to veto the bill twice.

In the 1950s, Dutch Elm disease began to kill the corridor of young trees just starting to shade the road. At the same time, construction of the New York State Thruway, closely paralleling the length of Route 5, eclipsed the old road once again. The drive to celebrate the Great Genesee Road died out with the elms. Even the Road of Memory became a memory.

Appendix A

Historical Markers

New York's Department of Education State History Office installed over 2,800 historical markers throughout the state. The program started in 1926 to commemorate the Sesquicentennial of the Revolutionary War. It was discontinued in 1966. Some of the signs have disappeared; occasionally a sign includes inaccurate information. Since 1966 local authorities have been responsible for the approval, installation, and maintenance of historical markers. The Pomeroy Foundation began awarding grants for signs in 2006, copying the state's blue-and-yellow design (but identified as Pomeroy). This is a listing primarily of original markers installed by the state, starting from Albany along the route of the old Genesee Road, Route 5, and the northern spur of the Seneca Turnpike.

Location: Broadway at foot of State St., Albany
Inscription: Henry Hudson
Explorer, Here Ended the Voyage of the Half Moon in Quest of the Indies, September 1609

Location: Broadway at foot of State St., Albany
Inscription: Birthplace of American Union
Near this site, Benjamin Franklin presented the 1st Formal Plan of National Union; Congress of 1754.

Location: Broadway at foot of State St., Albany
Inscription: Called Fort Nassau 1614
Fort Orange 1624, Beverwyck 1652, Albany 1664; Chartered 1686.

Location: Broadway at foot of State St., Albany
Inscription: Fort Orange
Site of West India Company Colony 1624. Fort Was Located to the Southeast by the River.

Location: Broadway at foot of State St., Albany
Inscription: Clermont
Near the foot of Madison Ave. Robert Fulton, in Aug. 1807, completed the first successful steamboat voyage.

Location: Broadway at foot of State St., Albany
Inscription: Colonial Warpath
Rendezvous of Troops in Five Wars. Here Armies Under Abercrombie, Loudoun and Amherst Moved to the Conquest of Canada 1756–60.

Location: Capitol Park, Eagle and State Streets, Albany
Inscription: Fort Frederick
In the Middle of this Street to the East stood Fort Frederick, Goal of Burgoyne's Drive to Split the Colonies—1777.

Location: Washington Ave. near Eagle St., Albany
Inscription: Birthplace of Modern Electricity
Here Discovering Magnetic Induction, Joseph Henry Pioneered the Telegraph and Electric Motor, 1829–31.

Location: Washington Ave. near Swan St., Albany
Inscription: General George Washington
Traveled This Road on His Tours of the Mohawk Valley 1782 and 1783.

Location: Maiden Lane between Eagle and Lodge Streets, Albany

Inscription: Schenectady Gate

Near This Point the Path to Schenectady Used by Indians and Fur Traders Led through the Palisades Which Enclosed the City.

Location: Capitol Park, Eagle St. near Washington Ave.

Inscription: The Capitol

Of the State of New York. Second Capitol Building Erected by the State. Cornerstone Laid 1871. 25 Years in Construction.

Location: Central Ave. near Northern Blvd., Albany

Inscription: Pioneer Route

At This Point the Pioneers Going West in Ox Carts and Horse Drawn Caravans Assembled. This Street Formerly Called the Bowery.

Location: Route 5 at eastern limit of Schenectady

Inscription: Albany Path

Ska-nek-ta-de Trail Through Open Pines. Wagon, Stagecoach and Military Road, Now State St. and Route 5 To Albany.

Note of Correction: This more properly describes Kings Road, not Route 5.

Location: Intersection of State St. and Washington Ave., Schenectady

Inscription: Canada 1760

Amherst With 6000 Americans, 4000 British & 200 Boats Marched via Mohawk & Oswego to Capture of Montreal, Sept. 8, 1760.

Location: Intersection of State St. and Washington Ave., Schenectady

Inscription: Clinton's Expedition

June 11, 1779 Left with 1500 Men & 200 Batteaux for Sullivan Campaign against Iroquois.

Location: Washington Ave., Schenectady

Inscription: Robert Sanders

House 1750. Washington Visited Here in 1775. Later Became Schenectady Female Academy

Location: End of Washington Ave., Schenectady

Inscription: Early Bridge

Wooden Suspension Bridge Erected Here 1808. Designed by Theodore Burr. Used by Saratoga Ry., 1832–39. Replaced 1874

Location: Glen Ave. at intersection with Route 5, Scotia.

Inscription: Glen Sanders House, 1713.

Built by Capt. Johannes Glen Partly of Materials in First Mohawk Valley House Built by Alexander Glen, 1655.

Note: The house is part of a modern hotel and events complex.

Location: Route 5 at Collins Park, Scotia.

Inscription: Abraham Glen

House 1730. Built by Abraham Glen Where King's Highway Left Mohawk River.

Location: Route 5 at Collins Park, Scotia.

Inscription: Mohawk Turnpike

Colonial Highway Westward to St. Johnsville Known as "King's Highway" Military Road, 1812

Location: Route 5 about one and one-half miles east of Hoffmans

Inscription: Josias Swart

Homestead Called the Sixth Flat. Josias Swart, b. 1653, Received a Deed from the Trustees of Schenectady, August 5, 1713.

Location: Route 5 near Hoffmans

Inscription: A Notable Home

Here About 1720 Stood the First House in This Part of the Valley, Home of Seven Generations of the Van Eps Family.

Location: Route 5, Hoffmans

Inscription: Hoffmans Ferry

Here About 1790 Harmanus Vedder Established a Ferry Which Bore His Name Until 1835 When the Ferry Rights Were Bought by J. Hoffman.

Location: Route 5 near Schenectady–Montgomery County Line

Inscription: Cement Mill

Here, 1825–45, Stood the Kiln and Mill of John Van Eps & Sons, Making the First Hydraulic Cement in This Part of the State.

Location: Route 5 about two and one-half miles east of Cranesville

Inscription: A Famous Inn

Here, 1795–1845, Stood the Hotel of John Van Eps Who Fought at Oriskany. Here Commodore Perry and Other Notables Were Entertained.

Location: Route 5 about two miles east of Cranesville

Inscription: Compaanen Kill

Near Here, According to Tradition, Is the Grave of Copaan the Oneida, Who at West Canada Creek, 1781, Tomahawked Walter Butler.

Location: Route 5, Cranesville

Inscription: Evaskill

Named After Mrs. Eva Van Alstyne Who Was Scalped Here 1755.

Location: Route 5, Cranesville

Inscription: Adriucha

De Groot Family Settled Here About 1700, Mill Built About 1710.

Location: Route 5, east edge of Amsterdam

Inscription: Old Manny Inn

Was on Lot 8, Sub-division of Lot 1 of the 13th Patent. Sold to Gabriel Manny 1804. Came into Possession of Ross Family in 1839.

Location: Route 5, Amsterdam

Inscription: Guy Park 1766

Built By Sir William Johnson for Daughter Molly, Wife of Col. Guy Johnson. Johnsons Left for Canada in 1775.

Location: Route 5, western edge of Amsterdam

Inscription: 200 Feet S.

Claus Mansion Built 1762 by Sir Wm. Johnson for His Daughter Nancy, Stood Between River and Present Railroad.

Location: Route 5, Fort Johnson

Inscription: Fort Johnson 1749

Third Mohawk Valley House Built by Sir William Johnson. Important Military Post and Indian Council Place of 1754–60

Location: Route 5, three miles east of Fonda

Inscription: Danascara Place

Built 1795 by Col. Frederick Vischer Replacing House Which Was Burned in the Valley Raid of 1780.

Location: Route 5, Fonda

Inscription: Approaching Site of Old

Caughnawaga Church Erected in 1763.

Location: Route 5, Fonda

Inscription: Davis Tavern

Famous in Days of Stage Coach Travel. Built About 1781 by Matthew C. Davis.

Location: Route 5, Fonda

Inscription: Van Horn House

Built by Abram Van Horn in 1826. Used as a Bakery and Store.

Location: Route 5, Fonda
Inscription: Fonda Tavern
Built About 1781 by John Fonda of Tryon County Militia.

Location: Route 5 one-half mile west of Fonda
Inscription: Liberty Pole
Erected on this Spot, Occasioned the First Blood Shed in Old Tryon County in May 1775.

Location: Route 5 one mile west of Fonda
Inscription: Veeder Home
Built About 1791 by Major Abraham Veeder Who Kept an Inn Here and Operated a Ferry across the River.

Location: West of Fonda
Inscription: Caughnawagae
Lower Mohawk Indian Castle 1667 Ruled by Turtle Clan. Jesuit Mission of St. Peter's Destroyed in Raid of 1693.

Location: Route 5 five miles west of Fonda
Inscription: Connolly Inn
Stood at Yosts Where There Was a Toll Gate and a Bridge Across the Mohawk Which Was Swept Away by High Water and Never Rebuilt.

Location: Route 5 four miles east of Palatine Bridge
Inscription: Site of the Early Home of Major Jelles Fonda, a Prominent Merchant by the Mohawk Valley and an Indian Trader. Here Was Located an Indian Village.

Location: Route 5 two miles east of Palatine Bridge
Inscription: Sprakers Inn
Built in 1795 by the Spraker Family. Once a Famous River and Turnpike Tavern.

Location: Route 5, Palatine Bridge

Inscription: Settled by Hendrick Frey 1689

Bridge Built 1803. Village Chartered 1867. Settled by Palatine Germans 1689–1867.

Note of correction: The 1689 date of settlement is two decades early.

Location: Route 5, Palatine Bridge

Inscription: Fort Frey 1739

Home of Maj. John Frey. Hendrick Frey Location at Foot of Hill 1689. British Fort Nearby 1701–1713.

Location: Route 5 one mile west of Nelliston

Inscription: Fort Wagner

Stone Section of House was Stockaded Home of Lt. Col. Peter Wagner, Palatine Regt. Tryon County Militia 1750.

Location: Route 5 at Palatine Church

Inscription: Army Camp of Gen. Van Rensselaer's American Army, Oct. 19, 1780. Also Site of Palatine Church 1770.

Location: Route 5 east of St. Johnsville

Inscription: 300 Feet N. (arrow)

Site of Reformed Church 1750. First Church Organization in Town of St. Johnsville.

Location: Route 5 at LeRoy Village line

Inscription: Ft. Hendrick

1754–1760 British Post Guarding Mohawk Castle. Named For King Hendrick Killed at Lake George, Sept. 1755.

Location: Route 5 about four miles west of Herkimer

Inscription: New Petersburgh Fort

A Stockade Built and Used by the Pioneers of Schuyler Prior to and during the American Revolution.

Location: Route 5 about five miles west of Herkimer

Inscription: Site of Home

Heinrich Staring, b. 1730–d. 1808. Captain 4th Regiment Tryon County Militia and 1st Judge of Court of Common Pleas of Herkimer County.

Location: Genesee Street at Main St., Utica

Inscription: Bagg's Tavern

Originally a Log House Founded 1794 by Moses Bagg. Washington, La Fayette, Henry Clay & Gen. Grant Were Guests Here

Location: Route 5 at intersection with Route 12, New Hartford

Inscription: Jedediah Sanger

Founded New Hartford in 1788 by Purchasing 1000 Acres of Land and Settling Here with His Family.

Location: Route 5 at intersection with Route 12, New Hartford

Inscription: 1st Religious Society of the Town of Whitestown, Organized 1791. Church Dedicated Nov. 29, 1797.

Location: Route 5, Oneida Castle

Inscription: Oneida Castle

Chief Village of Oneida Tribe of Indians, Members of Iroquois Confederacy.

Location: Route 5 two miles west of Canastota

Inscription: Quality Hill Green

A Company of Horse Artillery Drilled Here during the War of 1812.

Location: Parker Lane, Chittenango, near intersection of Routes 5 and 13

Inscription: Lateral Canal

Company Incorporated 1818. Canal in Use by 1824. Site of Turn-around Basin for Canal Boat Transportation North to the Grand Old Erie.

Location: Route 92, Manlius
Inscription: The First Schoolhouse
In the Town of Manlius Was Built of Logs and Stood Near Here in 1798.

Location: Route 5, Fayetteville
Inscription: Fayetteville
First Called "Manlius Four Corners." Settled in 1791 by Origen Eaton and Joshus Knowlton. Boyhood Home of Grover Cleveland.

Location: Route 5, Fayetteville
Inscription: Grover Cleveland
President of United States 1884–1888 and 1892–1896. His Boyhood Home Is the First House on the Left North of the Corner House.

Location: Route 5 at Walnut St., Fayetteville
Inscription: Matilda Joslyn Gage
Nationally Known Abolition and Women's Rights Advocate Lived Here from 1854 Until Her Death in 1898.

Location: Route 5, Dewitt
Inscription: Morehouse Flats
Benj. Morehouse Settled Here 1789. His Log Tavern Opened 1790. Mexico Town Organized Here 1791. Meeting Here Proposed Formation of Onondaga County Dec 23, 1793.

Location: Route 5, Dewitt
Inscription: John Young
1752–1834. Revolutionary Soldier. First Settler Here in 1791. Village First Called Youngsville.

Location: Route 5, Fairmount, two miles west of Syracuse
Inscription: Site of Home of James Geddes 1798
Erie Canal Surveyor 1808, Chief Engineer 1816–1825.

Location: Route 5, Elbridge

Inscription: Built About 1820

Home of Col. John Stevens, Onondaga County Militia, War of 1812.

Location: Route 5, Elbridge

Inscription: This Lot

Was Part of Military Tract of Capt. Wm. Stevens, Member Mass. Society Cincinnati. State Superintendent of Salt Industry.

Location: Route 5, Onondaga/Cayuga County line west of Elbridge

Inscription: Cayuga County

Early Iroquois Country 1768. Part of Montgomery Co. 1784. Part of Herkimer Co. 1791. Part of Onondaga Co. 1794. Cayuga Co. set off 1799.

Location: Route 5 east of Sennett

Inscription: Early Home

Built About 1795 by Daniel Sennett, Side Judge of Circuit Court. Town Named in His Honor.

Location: Turnpike Rd., Sennett

Inscription: Blacksmith Shop

Built Prior to 1825. Local Methodist Society Here Organized and Planned Erection of Their Church.

Location: Turnpike Rd., Sennett

Inscription: Baptist Church

Organized 1779. First Stone Church Built on This Site 1808. Present Church Built 1825.

Location: Turnpike Rd., Sennett

Inscription: Oldest Church in Sennett.

Built 1820. Organized 1809 as First Congregational. Remodeled 1847. Became Presbyterian 1870.

Location: Northeast corner Sennett four-corners

Inscription: First Store

in Village of Sennett opened 1795 by Rufus Sheldon and Chauncey Lathrop. First Post Office 1806.

Location: Route 173 one-half mile east of Jamesville

Inscription: Union Congregational Church

Building Erected 1808. Society Moved to Jamesville 1828.

Location: Route 173 about four miles east of Manlius (at Madison/Onondaga County line

Inscription: Deep Spring

Te-ungh-sat-ayagh, 450 Ft. North on Iroquois Trail. First Road Made 1790 by Gen. James Wadsworth. County Line and Survey Mark.

Location: Academy St., Manlius

Inscription: Cherry Valley Turnpike

Terminated Here. Completed About 1809, Joining the Seneca Turnpike Here.

Location: Route 173, Manlius

Inscription: Christ Church

Oldest Church Edifice and Oldest Episcopal Parish in Onondaga County. Inc. 1804, 1811. Built 1813. Removed to This Side 1832.

Location: Route 173, Manlius

Inscription: Gen. John J. Peck

Born Here Jan. 4, 1821; Won Promotion for Gallantry Mexican War. Made Maj. Gen. 1862. Defended Suffolk, Va. Died Syracuse, April 21, 1878.

Location: Route 173 one-half mile east of Onondaga Hill

Inscription: War of 1812

Captain Henry Crouch and Captain Benjamin Branch, Soldiers of War of 1812, Who Died While Encamped Near Here Are Buried Above.

Location: Route 175, Onondaga Hill

Inscription: Francis Asbury

First Bishop of the Methodist Episcopal Church Preached June 26, 1807 in Onondaga Court House Then Standing on This Site.

Location: Route 175, Marcellus

Inscription: Site of Tavern

Kept by Deacon Samuel Rice 1800. First Church Services Were Held Here, Also Town Meetings.

Location: Route 175, Marcellus

Inscription: First Sawmill

In Town of Marcellus Built 1796 by Deacon Samuel Rice and Judge Dan Bradley.

Location: Route 175, Marcellus

Inscription: Site of First Frame House

In Town of Marcellus. Built by Dr. Elnathan Beach, Who Served in American Revolution. Sheriff of County from 1799 to 1801.

Location: Route 175, Marcellus

Inscription: Site of First Church Edifice

In Onondaga County, Completed 1803. Present Church Built 1851

Location: Franklin St. Road (C.R. 133) four miles east of Auburn

Inscription: Great Genesee Road

Great Genesee Road from Old Fort Schuyler io the Genesee River via Hardenbergh Corners and Cayuga Bridge. Built 1794.

Note: The date refers to when the road was officially called "Great."

Location: Franklin St. Road three miles east of Auburn

Inscription: Blacksmith Shop

Built about 1837. First Trip Hammer in Cayuga County and First One Used in Auburn Prison Made Here.

Location: Franklin St., Auburn

Inscription: Calvary Presbyterian Church

Oldest Church Edifice in Auburn. Erected 1815–17 at Franklin and North Sts. as First Pres. Church Moved Here 1869.

Location: E. Genesee St., Auburn

Inscription: Francis Hunter Tavern

Francis Hunter Erected Tavern Here 1808 Under Nearby Elm. Councils Were Held Between White Settlers and Indians.

Location: E. Genesee St., Auburn

Inscription: First Freight Depot

Auburn and Syracuse R.R. Built by C. W. Pomeroy 1836. Building Used Later as Genesee Opera House.

Location: E. Genesee St., Auburn

Inscription: Wm. G. Fargo

May 20, 1818–Aug. 3, 1881. Organizer of Wells-Fargo Express Company Served Here as First Freight Agent.

Location: Genesee St. near Owasco Outlet Bridge, Auburn

Inscription: Site of First Log Dam and Mill

on Owasco River Built by John L Hardenbergh 1793. Enlarged 1802. Present Stone Mill 1824.

Location: Genesee St., Auburn

Inscription: First Tavern and Store

Opened in a Log Cabin Built by Samuel Bristol 1796.

Location: Genesee at North St., Auburn

Inscription: Pioneer Roads

Old Genesee Road 1791. New Genesee Road 1797. Old Chenango Road 1791 Later Known as Cayuga and Seneca Turnpike 1802.

Note: The dates are arbitrary.

Location: Genesee at Exchange St., Auburn
Inscription: Site of Bostwick's Tavern 1803–1868
Rebuilt 1824, Renamed Western Exchange Hotel. Lafayette a Guest 1825.

Location: Genesee St., Auburn
Inscription: Center House
Early Tavern Erected 1805 at Genesee and Market Sts. Moved Here 1829.

Location: Genesee St., Auburn
Inscription: Site of Willard Tavern 1810
Rebuilt 1828–1830 as American Hotel, Burned 1879.

Location: Genesee St. on Court House Green, Auburn
Inscription: Cayuga County Court House
Frame Building Erected on Rear of This Lot 1809. Present Building Erected 1836, Reconstructed 1922–24.

Location: W. Genesee St., Auburn
Inscription: Barracks
During the War of 1812 Barracks Were Established in This Locality. Troops Passing to and from Niagara Camped Here.

Location: Bayard St. two miles east of Seneca Falls
Inscription: Bridgeport
Formerly Cayuga Ferry & W. Cayuga Terminus of State Line. Bridge Prominent When Auburn Was "Hardenbergh's Corner."
Note: Terminus of state line?

Location: Bayard St. one-half mile east of Seneca Falls
Inscription: Old Genesee Stage Route
Cayuga Lake Bridge Made This the Main Route Until the Erie Canal of 1822 and the Railway of 1840.

Location: Bayard St. one-half mile east of Seneca Falls

Inscription: Potter Inn Farm

Nathaniel J. Potter, Innkeeper, Blacksmith on Genesee Road, 1801–1808. His Son Henry Potter Lived Here, 1st Pres. Western Union Telegraph, 1851.

Location: Route 5, corner of Mynderse St., Seneca Falls

Inscription: First Convention for Women's Rights Was Held on This Corner 1848.

Location: Route 5, Seneca Falls

Inscription: Mynderse Academy

Named for Col. Wilhelmus Mynderse, Founder of Seneca Falls.

Location: W. Bayard at Sackett Street, Seneca Falls

Inscription: Home of Gary V. Sackett 1790–1885

Judge, Court of Common Pleas. Promoter of Canal System.

Location: Route 5 between Seneca Falls and Waterloo

Inscription: Along North Side of River

Marched Sullivan's Forces Expedition Commanded by Col. Peter Gansevoort & Lt. Col. William Butler Sept. 20–21, 1779.

Location: Route 5 one mile east of Waterloo

Inscription: Kingdom Cemetery

Reserved in Deed to Thomas Lawrence. Here Until 1856 Were Mills, Distilleries, Taverns, School, Justice Ct., Masonic Lodge, Race Track.

Location: Waterloo, east end

Inscription: Military Route

Of the Sullivan-Clinton Army on its Campaign against the British and Indians of Western New York in 1779.

Location: S. Exchange St., Geneva
Inscription: Site of Log House
Erected 1787. Later Known as Clark Jennings Tavern.

Location: Washington St. between Pulteney and S. Main, Geneva
Inscription: Site of Geneva Hotel
Erected 1796 by Capt. Charles Williamson.
Note: Not just the "site of."

Location: Hamilton St. (Route 5) near Route 14 intersection, Geneva
Inscription: Site of Geneva Medical College
Eliz. Blackwell Received Here in 1849 the First Degree of Medicine Ever Conferred Upon a Woman.

Location: S. Main at Parrish St., Canandaigua
Inscription: Site of Pioneer Home
Capt. Jasper Parrish Settled Here in 1792. Indian Captive Six Years. Govt. Interpreter later. Died in 1826.

Location: N. Main St. at Public Square, Canandaigua
Inscription: Phelps Gorham Purchase
Pioneer Land Office in Western NY Estab. Here. 1st Judge of County 1789–93.

Location: Genesee St. (Route 5) at Route 15A, Lima
Inscription: Gandichiragou
"At the Forks of the Trail." Name Recorded 1634. Destroyed by De Nonville's French Army 1687. Site Also of Father Garnier's Chapel of St. Jean.

Location: Genesee St. at College Ave, Lima
Inscription: Genesee Wesleyan Seminary
Founded 1832. Genesee College Established 1849 and on April 14, 1869, Was Allowed to Remove to Form Syracuse University.

Location: Genesee St, Lima

Inscription: Warner House

Built by Ashahel Warner 1810, Who Was Pioneer in 1795. Used by Trinity Mark Masonic Lodge No. 59, 1810. Union Lodge No. 45, 1816.

Location: Route 5, Lima

Inscription: Site of Ska-hase-ga-o

(Was-a-long-creek) A Populous Modern Seneca Indian Village.

Location: Route 5 about three miles west of Avon

Inscription: John Hugh Mac Naughton 1826–1891

Lived Here 20 Years. Famous Poet and Song Writer.

Location: Route 5, Caledonia

Inscription: Big Springs

Ancient Indian Camp Site on Niagara Trail. Earliest White Tourist 1615. Scottish Settlers 1799. Terminus Pioneer RR. 1838.

Location: Route 5, Caledonia

Inscription: Erected 1826

By Major Gad Blakslee. Early Post Office, First Bank, Apothecary Shop, Now Caledonia Library.

Location: Route 5, Caledonia

Inscription: Erected 1827

By James R. Clark. Early Tavern, Post Office, Early Bank, Library. Certified by Historic American Buildings Survey.

Location: Route 5, Caledonia west end

Inscription: Caledonia

Organized 1803 as Town of Southampton. Name Changed to Caledonia 1806; Scottish Emigrants Settled 1799. Village Incorporated 1891.

Location: Route 5, eastern edge of LeRoy

Inscription: Ganson Tavern

First Settlement between Genesee River and Buffalo. Tavern Conducted by Charles Wilbur 1793, Capt. John Ganson 1797.

Location: E. Main St. (Route 5), LeRoy

Inscription: LeRoy House

Built Before 1812 as a Land Office for the Triangle Tract. Deeded to Union Free School District 1911.

Location: W. Main St. (Route 5), Batavia

Inscription: Seat of Holland Land Office

This City Was Founded in 1801 by Joseph Ellicott, Local Agent of Holland Land Company.

Location: Main St. (Route 5) near Garrison Rd., Williamsville

Inscription: U.S. Barracks 1812

Along Garrison Rd to Creek and Extending Southeast Were Log Barracks of Gen Smyth's Army During Winter of 1812 and '13. These buildings Were Later Used as Hospital.

Note: "These buildings" are no longer there.

Appendix B
Travel Tips

Crailo State Historic Site

9-1/2 Riverside Ave., Rensselaer

518-463-8738

parks.ny.gov/historic-sites/crailo/details.aspx

Across the river from Albany, a museum of Dutch Colonial history in the Hudson Valley is located in an eighteenth-century fort/home of the Rensselaer patroon family. Exhibits highlight the archeology of Fort Orange. Open May–Oct., Wed.–Sun.

New York State Capitol

State St. and Washington Ave., Albany

518-474-2418

Empirestateplaza.ny.gov

A tour through this huge, byzantine building is an adventure to remember, a panoply of grand staircases, intricate carvings, murals, colors of stone, hidden chambers. Four architects were involved, but H. H. Richardson is primarily credited with the Romanesque design. Open Mon.–Fri.; tours at 10, noon, and 2.

Albany Institute of History and Art

125 Washington Ave., Albany

518-463-4478

albanyinstitute.org

One of the oldest museums in the United States, established in 1791, but a modern facility and essential resource on the life and culture of the upper Hudson Valley. Open Wed.–Sat., 10–5 p.m., Sun., noon–5.

Albany Pine Bush Preserve

195 New Karner Rd., Albany

518-456-0655

albanypinebush.org

The Discovery Center (main building, on New Karner) is close to a rare section of old roadbed, part of a twenty-mile network of trails. Excellent map online. Open every day.

Schenectady History Museum

32 Washington Ave., Schenectady

518-374-0263

schenectadyhistorical.org

Located in an elegant mansion on the way to the old Mohawk River crossing, this is the place to get oriented exploring the fascinating Stockade District. Open Mon.– Fri., 10 –5 p.m., Sat. 10–2 p.m.

Old Fort Johnson

2 Mergner Rd., Fort Johnson (intersection of Routes 5 and 67W)

518-843-0300

oldfortjohnson.org

The most significant of the surviving eighteenth-century house/forts in the Mohawk Valley, with many stories to tell about Sir William. Call for house tour reservation. Visitor Center is in an old stable. Open Wed.–Sun., May 17–Oct. 15.

Tribes Hill Heritage Center

360 Mohawk Drive, Tribes Hill (Fonda)

518-829-4058

tribeshillheritagecenter.com

Native American artifacts collection, cultural and crafts center. Open Wed.–Sun.

Montgomery County History & Archives Department

9 Park Street, Fonda

518-853-8186

A trove of local and regional history located in Fonda's stunning, 1836 Old Courthouse. Sept.–June 8:30–4; July and Aug. 9–4.

Saint Kateri National Historic Shrine and Mohawk Caughnawaga Indian Museum

3636 Route 5, Fonda

518-853-3646

katerishrine.org

Chapel, spring, and grotto with hiking trails open year-round. Also a museum of artifacts and information about the nearby Mohawk village archaeological site.

Fort Klock Restoration

7203 Route 5, St. Johnsville

518-568-7779

fortklockrestoration.org

A thirty-acre complex includes a c. 1750 stone homestead, colonial Dutch barn, blacksmith shop, and schoolhouse. Call for hours and schedule of events.

Moss Island

Little Falls

An island park in the Mohawk created by a channel of the Erie Canal, this is a great place to see the dramatic rock formations of cascading falls, and view Lock 17, the tallest in the Barge Canal system.

Munson-Williams-Proctor Art Institute

310 Genesee Street, Utica

315-797-0000

munson.art

A stunning museum of art, performing arts center, and school of art. Open Tues.–Sat. 10–5; Sun. 12–5.

Oneida County Historical Society Museum

1608 Genesee St, Utica

315-735-3642

oneidacountyhistory.org

Open Tues.–Fri. 10–4:30. Sat. 11–3.

The Erie Canal Museum

318 Erie Blvd. East, Syracuse

315-471-0593

eriecanalmuseum.org

Located in an 1850 Weighlock Building, the last vestige of the canal as it once passed through downtown Syracuse. A fascinating look at the history, workings, and culture of the canal, including a full-size replica line boat. Check out how canal boats were weighed! Open daily 10–4.

Chittenango Falls State Park

2300 Rathbun Rd., Cazenovia

315-492-1756

parks.ny.gov/parks/130/

A half-mile trail loops around a 167-foot waterfall over the crest of the Onondaga Escarpment. About five miles south of Chittenango on Route 13, but worth the diversion.

Marcellus Historical Society/Tefft-Steadman House

18 North Street, Marcellus

315-673-4839

Marcellushistoricalsociety.org

Open Sun. 1–3 and Thurs. 1–4.

Seward House Museum

33 South Street, Auburn

315-252-1283

sewardhouse.org

The five-decade home of New York governor and Lincoln's secretary of state William H. Seward. One block from Genesee Street and a step back into the nineteenth century. Open Tues.–Sat. 10–5 p.m.

Cayuga Museum of History and Art

203 Genesee St., Auburn

315-253-8051

cayugamuseum.org

Main exhibits in the 1836 Willard-Case House. Open Wed.–Sat. 11–4. Case Research Lab tours (behind the house) on the hour, 11–3.

Women's Rights National Historical Park

136 Fall St., Seneca Falls

315-568-0024

nps.gov/wori

A museum complex celebrating the 1848 Seneca Falls Convention. The National Women's Hall of Fame is nearby, beside the canal in an imposing 1844 knitting factory (315-568-8080; womenofthehall.org). The park visitor center is open daily 9–5 p.m. Associated historic homes have differing hours.

Seneca Falls Historical Society

55 Cayuga St., Seneca Falls

315-568-8412

sfhistoricalsociety,square.site

A magnificent, twenty-three-room Victorian mansion open Mon.–Fri. 9–4 p.m.

Geneva History Museum

543 South Main St., Geneva

315-789-5151

Historicgeneva.org

The museum's Prouty-Chew House is part of the city's charming, original neighborhood. Open May 1–Oct. 31, Mon.–Sat. 9:30–4:30 p.m.; Nov. 1–Apr. 30, Tues.–Sat. 9:30–4:30.

Ontario County Historical Museum

55 North Main St., Canandaigua

585-394-4975

ochs.org

Open Tues.–Fri. 10–4:30 p.m., Sat., 11–3.

East Bloomfield Historical Society

8 South Ave., East Bloomfield

585-657-7244

ebhs1838.org

The collection includes thousands of local artifacts and a replica of a 1791 log schoolhouse. Call for appointment Wed.–Fri. 9–2 p.m.

Ganondogan State Historic Site

7000 County Rd. 41, Victor

585-924-5848

ganondagan.org

Not along the old road but well worth a detour; site of the largest seventeenth-century Seneca village. Art & Cultural Center open Wed.–Sat. 9–4 p.m. (Bark Longhouse May 1–Oct. 31).

LeRoy House and Jell-O Gallery Museum

23 East Main St., LeRoy

585-768-7433

leroyhistoricalsociety.org

Everything you could ever want to know about Jell-O and more; but don't miss the museum's lower floor for an unrelated, wonderful collection of vehicles that once traveled the old road. Open Apr. 27–Dec. 31 Thurs–Saturday 10–4 p.m.; Sunday 1–4. Call for hours for the historic house.

Holland Land Office Museum

131 West Main St., Batavia

585-343-4727

hollandlandoffice.com

A rich trove of Western New York history packed into a landmark 1815 stone land office (and newer wings). Open Tues.–Sat. 10–4 p.m.

Clarence Bike Path

www2.erie.gov/clarence/index.php?q=bike-path-information

For a break from driving, bike or walk along this rail path running through the village and another seven miles toward Buffalo. Parking and map around the corner on Salt Road, behind the 1810 hotel building.

Clarence History Museum

10465 Main St., Clarence

716-759-8575

clarencehistory.org

Located in the village's pretty memorial park, the museum is only open on second and fourth Sundays, 1–3 p.m., Mar.–Dec. A rare, 1820s log cabin at the site is a treat to see even when not open.

Broderick Park

1170 Niagara St., Buffalo (end of West Ferry St.)

Interpretive center, storyboards on the historic ferry landing, underground railroad terminus, and lift bridge over the canal.

Canalside

Buffalo waterfront.

At the foot of Buffalo's Main Street, where the oldest road across New York State comes to an end—a restored Lake Erie steamship wharf, riverside promenade, and a century-old carousel.

Selected Bibliography

Beers, F. W. *History of Montgomery and Fulton Counties, NY*. New York: F. W. Beers & Co., 1878.

Bigelow, Timothy. *Journal of a Tour to Niagara Falls in the Year 1805*. Boston: Press of John Wilson & Son, 1876.

Brodhead, John Romeyn. *History of the State of New York*. New York: Harper & Brothers, 1853.

Brumberg, G. David. *The Making of an Upstate Community*. Geneva, NY: Geneva Bicentennial Commission, 1976.

Buford, Mary Hunter. *Seth Read, Lieutenant-Colonel Continental Army: Pioneer at Geneva, New York, 1787, and at Erie, Penn., June 1795: His Ancestors and Descendants*. Boston: 1895.

Bushnell, David I., Jr. *Native Villages and Village Sites East of the Mississippi*. Washington, DC: Smithsonian Institution Bureau of American Ethnology, Bulletin 69, 1919.

Chazanoff, William. *Joseph Ellicott and the Holland Land Company: The Opening of Western New York*. Syracuse, NY: Syracuse University Press, 1970.

Clayton, W. W. *History of Onondaga County*. Syracuse, NY: D. Mason & Co., 1878.

Clune, Henry W. *The Genesee*. New York: Holt Rinehart Winston, 1963.

Conover, George S., ed. *A History of Ontario County, NY*. Syracuse, NY: D. Mason & Co., 1893.

Cooper, Susan Fennimore. *Missions to the Oneidas*. The Living Church, 1886.

Doty, Lockwood R. *A History of Livingston County, NY*. Geneseo, NY: E. E. Doty, 1876.

——, ed. *A History of the Treaty of Big Tree*. Dansville, NY: Livingston County Historical Society, 1896.

Dwight, Timothy. *Travels in New-England and New-York, Vol. III*. New Haven, CT: Timothy Dwight, 1822.

Ellicott, Joseph. *Reports of Joseph Ellicott as Chief of Survey (1797–1800): and as Agent (1800–1821) of the Holland Land Company's Purchases in Western New York*. Buffalo, NY: Buffalo Historical Society, 1937–41.

Flick, Alexander, ed. *History of the State of New York, Vol. 5, Conquering the Wilderness*. New York: Columbia University Press, 1934.

French, J. H. *Gazetteer of the State of New York*. Syracuse, NY: R. P. Smith, 1860.

Frey, Samuel Ludlow. *Frey Family Papers, General Manuscripts of Samuel Ludlow Frey*. Cooperstown, NY: New York State Historical Association Research Library, 1790–1917.

Graymont, Barbara. *The Iroquois in the American Revolution*. Syracuse, NY: Syracuse University Press, 1972.

Greene, Nelson. *The Old Mohawk Turnpike Book*. Fort Plain, NY: N. Greene, 1924.

——, ed., *History of the Mohawk Valley: Gateway to the West 1614–1925*. Chicago: S. J. Clarke Publishing Co., 1925.

Halsey, Francis Whiting. *The Old New York Frontier*. New York: Charles Scribner's Sons, 1901.

Hopkins, Joshua Victor. *Onondaga; or Reminiscences of Earlier and Later Times, Vol. II*. Syracuse, NY: Stoddard & Babcock, 1849.

Hulbert, Archer Butler. *Historic Highways of America, Vol. 12*. Cleveland: The Arthur H. Clark Co., 1902.

Isachsen, Y. W., Landing, E., Lauber, J. M., Rickard, L. V., and Rogers, W. B., eds. *Geology of New York*. Albany, NY: New York State Museum Educational Leaflet *28*, 2000.

Johanson, Bruce Elliott, and Barbara Alice Mann, eds. *Encyclopedia of the Haudenosaunee (Iroquois Confederacy)*. Westport, CT: Greenwood Press, 2000.

Kappler, Charles Joseph, ed. *Indian Affairs: Laws and Treaties, Vol. 2, Laws and Treaties*. Washington, DC: U.S. Senate, 1904.

Ketchum, William. *An Authentic and Comprehensive History of Buffalo, with Some Accounts of Its Early Inhabitants, Both Savage and Civilized, and Historic Notices of the Six Nations*. Buffalo, NY: Rockwell, Baker & Hill, 1865.

Leslie, Edmund Norman. *Skaneateles: History of Its Earliest Settlement and Reminiscences of Later Times*. New York: A. H. Kellogg, 1902.

Megapolensis, Johannes. *A Short Sketch of the Mohawk Indians in the New Netherland, Their Land, Stature, Dress, Manners, and Magistrates, Written in the Year 1644*. New York: New-York Historical Society, 1857.

Norton, A. Tiffany. *History of Sullivan's Campaign Against the Iroquois*. Lima, NY: 1879.

O'Callaghan, E. B., ed. *The Documentary History of the State of New-York, Vol. I-IV*. Albany, NY: Weed, Parsons & Co., 1849.

Parker, Arthur C. *The Code of Handsome Lake, the Seneca Prophet*. Albany, NY: University of the State of New York., 1913.

Pearson, Jonathan. *A History of the Schenectady Patent in the Dutch and English Times*. Albany, NY: J. Munsell's Sons, 1883.

Smith, H. Perry, ed. *History of the City of Buffalo and Erie County*. Syracuse, NY: D. Mason & Co., 1884.

Smith, James H. *History of Livingston County, New York*. Syracuse, NY: D. Mason & Co., 1881.

Trelease, Allen W. *Indian Affairs in Colonial New York*. Ithaca, NY: Cornell University Press, 1960.

Turner, Orsamus. *History of the Pioneer Settlement of Phelps and Gorham's Purchase and Morris' Reserve.* Rochester, NY: William Alling, 1851.

———, *Pioneer History of the Holland Purchase of Western New York.* Buffalo, NY: Jewett, Thomas & Co., 1849.

von Engeln, O. D. *The Finger Lakes Region: Its Origin and Nature.* Ithaca, NY: Cornell University Press, 1961.

Weissand, Patrick. *The Great Survey, 1998–1800 and the Life and Times of Joseph Ellicott.* Batavia, NY: Holland Purchase Historical Society, 2002.

Yates, Austin A. *Schenectady County, New York: Its History to the Close of the Nineteenth Century.* New York: New York History Co., 1902.

Index